The INVERSO Method

The INVERSO Method

Turning Your Finances Around

Marianela Inverso

MERIDIANA

Marianela Inverso
The INVERSO Method. Turning Your Finances Around

First edition, 2026
ISBN 978-987-3729-17-1

Published by Meridiana

Content

THE INVERSO TURN

There's one situation pilots fear more than almost any other. It has a vivid, sinister name: the graveyard spiral. When a plane flies into thick cloud, or through a night with no horizon, the pilot loses every visual reference. With no fixed point outside, the inner ear, the tiny organ that governs balance, begins to lie. If the plane banks slowly enough, the body never registers the tilt, and the pilot feels the plane is flying level while it is really turning and dropping into a spiral that winds tighter and tighter toward the ground. As it starts to descend, instinct screams at the pilot to pull back on the controls and climb. But the plane is banked, so pulling back only tightens the spiral and speeds the fall. Instinct leads straight to disaster, and it has killed a great many people.

What is the only way out? Do the opposite of what your body is asking for. Ignore your own sensations and trust the instruments on the panel, which coldly report the plane's real position even when you feel otherwise. The trained pilot learns that in disorientation it is instinct that sinks you, and that righting the plane means reversing the impulse, letting go of what fear demands and steering by something other than your own feeling.

Something very similar happens with money. We inherit a gut way of reacting that often pulls us into the spiral instead of out of it: fear makes us sell at the worst possible moment, distress makes us spend to calm down. Like the disoriented pilot, we tend to do the very thing that sinks us, only harder. This book is largely about learning to recognize when instinct is fooling us, and to trust the instruments we build in calmer moments rather than going blind in the panic of the now.

Personal finance often shows up as the poor relation of economics, a minor matter you settle with a little discipline and a tidy spreadsheet. Yet it sits at the center of a remarkable zone where the great structural forces of markets and technology braid with our most intimate decisions. Personal finance begins exactly where macroeconomics turns into biography. It is a crowded and often confusing territory, increasingly populated by salespeople promising certainty in exchange for attention. Courses on crypto and fast-return trading promise "financial freedom" and reinforce the old, worthy belief in financial literacy: with enough information and a few well-chosen indicators, uncertainty can be made to vanish.

That promise, when it is not an outright con, rests on the assumption that we will apply what we learn consistently and rationally over time, as if the whole problem were one of knowledge. In practice, the opposite tends to happen: we absorb intricate ideas about digital assets and technical analysis and then trade under pressure, every which way. We may have information and technical know-how to spare, but without the capacity to hold a coherent line in emotionally demanding moments, we end up no better off than before.

Financial literacy gets sold as the master key, and it falls short for two main reasons. The first is that it is framed as a technical matter handled by stable, coherent people who never lose their motivation, when in fact we decide while tired, tangled in family troubles and fears, inside the storm of emotion that runs through any human life. The second is that traditional financial literacy is bound to a world of scarce information and slow markets, where decisions got made in neutral surroundings. That world is no longer ours.

The environment in which we now make financial decisions is built to overwhelm that rationality. Twenty years ago, buying something meant leaving the house and handing physical cash to a shopkeeper, and every step along the way was a chance to think again. Today a notification offers you the thing you wanted to buy yesterday, at the price your search history suggests you would be willing to pay, one click away. Lending apps approve in minutes the kind of loan that used to take weeks of paperwork. The whole environment pushes us to decide fast, if not necessarily well.

The INVERSO Method is an answer to these challenges. It works through an architecture of systems built to move with our nature rather than against it, anticipating our moments of weakness and placing the important decisions in the right settings rather than leaving them to the exhaustion of late evening.

The method's name folds several meanings into one. It points, first, to its author's surname. It also points to the craft of investing money well. Above all, it names the act of turning over what has been set down wrong. Inverting the starting point, to begin with. Instead of opening with technique (the way the whole tradition does), we open with the person and their identity, which is where financial decisions are really made. Deeper still, the method inverts in the pilot's sense, the one who rights the plane. Much of our relationship with money runs backward without our having chosen it, inherited and governed by instinct and fear. This path lets us escape the old lament of personal finance, the one that mourns abandoned discipline while never building the conditions that would have prevented the problem.

Each letter represents one layer of the method. Together they form a coherent structure. Seen up close they look independent, yet each layer shapes the others and is shaped by them in turn. In that continuous interaction, a sum of parts becomes a living structure.

I takes up financial identity, the starting point that usually stays offstage. It is where personal history, learned patterns, inherited fears, and the narratives we absorbed without noticing all twine together and work in silence every time we make a financial decision. More than an inward exercise, it means recognizing that every financial strategy rests on someone who decides, and that someone is quite specific. Without understanding who decides, and what they fear and habitually do, any strategy, however sophisticated, runs aground sooner or later.

N sets the north: clear goals anchored in our own lives. What we want hardens from a vague aspiration into a structure with deadlines and room for adjustment, built to withstand the pressures of life, with its disorderly weeks and good and bad runs. A north well drawn can be redrawn without losing its meaning.

V calls for radical visibility, for seeing what actually happens to our money, with no blind spots. Plenty of decisions get made on incomplete perceptions and end in disaster. Visibility lights up the opaque areas, and the clarity that comes from steady, non-obsessive attention keeps blind spots from quietly skewing decisions we believe we are making freely.

E takes on strategy through simple designs, matched to your time horizon and your tolerance for risk, made to withstand both the volatility of the market and the volatility of our emotions. Instead of trusting luck or sudden inspiration, we will build solid structures that can hold up when the storm comes. The best portfolio is the one that will not leave us without a boat in the middle of the crossing.

R examines emotional risk, bringing in a variable usually treated as an occasional detour when in fact it is structural. We never decide in a vacuum or guided by concepts alone: we decide surrounded by haste, fear, euphoria, or fatigue, with all of it on our backs. We have to anticipate those states and build them into the design. This does not mean eliminating emotional risk, which is impossible, but once we know its patterns we can build mechanisms that soften the blow when it arrives.

S develops the security we need to live without constant alarm, and widens the usual notion of protection to get there. We will build an environment that can absorb contingencies and let us live without the feeling of existential threat around every corner. No security plan removes life's tragedies, but softening their consequences is no small thing, above all at the very moment we have to live through them.

O, finally, is about orchestration across the personal, the couple, and the family, where financial decisions reveal, and sometimes strain, the shared emotional choreographies. Here the system reaches maturity, because we move from managing money to coordinating multiple kinds of capital: time, professional skills, relationships, physical health, emotional energy. Financial decisions show up here as part of a wider dynamic that turns one kind of resource into another, even when we had not planned on it. Orchestration lets us do that consciously, by deliberate design.

By this route, the INVERSO Method builds a relationship with money that feeds our peace of mind and our dignity, one that holds up over time and adapts to the ever more complex settings that test us. Today's algorithms anticipate and shape our decisions; isolation and naive resistance are not workable strategies; better to put our energy into designing systems that can coexist with that reality without surrendering autonomy. Impossible controls only curdle into frustration and discouragement. We start instead from how we actually are and orchestrate, out of everything we have, a melody worth hearing. The INVERSO turn comes down, in the end, to this: we stop reacting to whatever lands in front of us and take command of our decisions, with ideas about money built for the world we live in.

I

Identity

Before we talk about money, we have to talk about history. The numbers and budgets will come soon enough. For now, let's look at our own past. Every financial decision belongs to a longer path, and when we manage money we are surrounded by economic experiences and wounds we often can't name or trace to their source. With those ghosts circling, any goal we set will be an illusion. The letter I is about our identity in relation to money, and it helps us identify those ghosts and finally show them the door.

Let's start with a story. Some time ago, a young man I'll call T. told me he had learned that money was a very serious thing, and not at school, much less at his first job. It happened one morning when he was eight, while his mother went over the electricity bill as if it were a hieroglyph from a lost civilization. She didn't say a word, but her shoulders rose an inch or two and her finger traced a circle over a number, as if trying to pin down an uncomfortable truth.

T. repeated the gesture with his own finger over the imaginary number, looked at me as if surfacing back into the present, and told me that in that instant he understood that adults could face monsters in the dark and yet feel helpless in front of numbers that arrived in the mail. They never talked about it, but his mind kept a silent, persistent note. Over the years, T. became good at a thousand things, just not at handling his money. He worked, studied, earned his first paycheck, and every month he replayed the scene: the receipt in hand, the lift of the shoulders, the circle over the uncomfortable number, with the same emotional choreography he had watched as a child.

Each of us has a choreography like that, some more pronounced than others. Some people get families where saving is survival; others grow up spending to celebrate being alive, or caught between heavy silences and entangled pride and fear. Each case leaves its mark on the emotions that run us. The good news is that recognizing the bias behind these stories is the first step toward loosening its grip, disabling the autopilot that sometimes has us tracing circles in the air without getting anywhere.

1. The Psychology of Money and the Six Emotional Signatures

We're used to hearing that managing money is a purely rational skill, as if knowing how to add and subtract were enough to make sensible decisions. Human behavior, unfortunately, laughs at that idea. Herbert Simon won the Nobel Prize in Economics in 1978 for breaking with the dominant model: people, he argued, don't optimize. They satisfice, settling for the first option that's good enough. The *homo oeconomicus*, that ideal agent who weighs every available option and always picks the best one, describes no one in real life.[1] We do the reverse. We take the first option that clears a minimum threshold of acceptability and stop there, because optimizing demands complete information, unlimited time, and cognitive energy, all things we are always short of. Behavioral economics, the study of how decisions actually get made, was built on this idea.

[1] Herbert Simon, "A Behavioral Model of Rational Choice," Quarterly Journal of Economics 69.1 (1955): 99–118.

Soon after, Richard Thaler and Hersh Shefrin described personal finance as a conflict between an impulsive self that wants gratification now and a planning self that promises order tomorrow, a conflict the more rational party doesn't always win.[2] Daniel Kahneman, the 2002 Nobel laureate, and Amos Tversky studied how people weigh losses against gains and found that an overwhelming share of economic decisions run on emotional shortcuts.[3] We fear losing more than we want to win. We blow some risks out of proportion and wave others away for immediate relief, even when it costs us later.

The very idea of the 'rational individual' comes apart once calculation and optimization give way to improvisation, but we shouldn't rush to a diagnosis of low intelligence. Plenty of brilliant, thoughtful people keep making irrational decisions.[4] And still we keep hearing that we ought to be logical about money, that discipline is all it takes.

If we can't count on clear access to our own motives, we need an approach that doesn't lose itself cataloguing kinds of neurosis or personality traits in general. We need one that picks out stable, money-specific patterns, what we will call financial signatures. These are emotional modes, learned patterns that surface when we are stressed or confused, exactly when our decisions about money carry the most weight.

These six signatures come out of research on loss aversion, affective buying, chronic financial avoidance, optimism bias, perfectionism, excessive control, and the patterns of emotional rescue that run inside families, what the literature calls financial enabling. They amount to a serious gallery of how the human mind behaves once money walks on stage. Every one of them works to

---

[2]Richard Thaler and Hersh Shefrin, "An Economic Theory of Self-Control," Journal of Political Economy 89.2 (1981): 392–406.

[3]Daniel Kahneman and Amos Tversky, "Prospect Theory: An Analysis of Decision under Risk," Econometrica 47.2 (1979): 263–292.

[4]Richard Thaler, Misbehaving: The Making of Behavioral Economics (London: Penguin, 2015); and Dan Ariely, Predictably Irrational (London: Harper, 2008).

lower emotional discomfort in the short run, even when that breeds trouble in the long run.

Almost all of us have a primary signature and a secondary one that surfaces when things get hard. Knowing yours better hands you better tools for whatever comes, and it changes your relationship with money by revealing why certain mistakes and loops keep repeating. There are no good or bad signatures, strictly speaking, yet any of them, pushed out of range, can cause real suffering. This is where the INVERSO Method begins, reworking our finances without asking us to become someone we are not.

The Accumulator

The Accumulator rarely stars in dramatic scenes about money. Nothing flares up where others can see it, because this person's relationship with money is quiet, a background tension that shadows every decision without ever becoming fully explicit. When the paycheck lands, relief arrives, dry and functional, almost clerical, carrying no sense of achievement, more a confirmation that the system is still running.

That same uneasy weather hangs over every expense, needed or not, always shadowed by worry about financial storms that might be coming. Even with no concrete threat in view, the vague need to hold on to what they have colors everything, and a near-primitive caution takes over. The Accumulator isn't exactly cheap. He is able to enjoy things, but what rules them is a deep aversion to loss.[5] The familiar always feels safer. So they compare, check balances, lean toward the conservative option, and put off, always, the thing they would actually enjoy. Life hangs suspended in a prudence that looks reasonable from outside and is very hard to live from within.

The strength of this signature is plain, and often genuinely valuable: discipline, a resistance to impulse. But it comes with an

[5]For a detailed account, see H. Shefrin and R. Thaler, Beyond Greed and Fear: Understanding Behavioral Finance and the Psychology of Investing (Boston: Harvard Business School Press, 2000).

emotional rigidity that holds the body in a low, unbroken state of alert. The Accumulator keeps a running tally of every number, a small wall against the unpredictable, at the risk that constant vigilance crowds out experience and drains the pleasure from life.

The Compensator

For the Compensator, buying isn't really about objects. The 'Add to cart' button becomes a fast, socially sanctioned form of mild anesthesia, a hit of momentary relief. This person buys because something inside is making noise and no other quick way to quiet it is at hand. The noise can show up as tiredness, a run of small frustrations, or the blurry sense of always chasing something just ahead. It doesn't take a crisis. A rough week can be enough, the kind that seems to heal with a purchase.

The purchase, then, is an emotional reply that suspends rational judgment. Faced with an appealing prompt to buy, the dopamine system kicks in, which is why so many 'unnecessary' purchases feel urgent in the moment, wrapped in a sense of deserving it and a chance that won't come again. The rationalizing arrives afterward, once the effect has already started to fade.

The Compensator tends to buy alone, often late at night, when the outside noise drops and the inside noise rises. The packages arrive afterward almost as if no one had ordered them, piling up like relics of an urgency that quickly faded away. Still, to file this person under impulsiveness would be unfair. The Compensator has a real gift the other signatures lack: the ability to enjoy without chaining everything to some endless 'later,' and yet the relief runs almost entirely through consumption, with money working like a painkiller that never reaches the thing underneath. Rigid bans and moral lectures get nowhere here; what works is learning to meet the discomfort before it converts into a purchase, building ways to settle yourself that don't always route through the card.

The Avoider

If some people deal with stress by staring at their statements, others do the reverse. The Avoider doesn't look. Rather than incapacity or indifference; money simply occupies an uncomfortable or secondary spot in their experience. Each time a review or a decision comes due, a feeling of overload rises, a sense of energy spent for no good reason. Avoidance here is an automatic form of regulation, not negligence.

Sometimes this is learned early, in homes where the accounts came bundled with sharp arguments or a steady hum of anxiety, so that facing the numbers head-on got welded to distress. Other times there's no clear episode at all: money isn't tied to any sharp anguish, but it isn't central either. The attention goes to work, to family, to creative or intellectual projects, to whatever feels more urgent, and the financial side slides into the background. People tend to ignore whatever demands high mental effort for little expected payoff.[6] Like any task that demands focus and precision, managing money carries a mental cost, and the Avoider lowers that cost by tending only to the indispensable. Each deferral brings brief relief that reinforces the habit. The trouble is that financial time never stops: the decisions we put off quietly become decisions made by default. What a small adjustment could have fixed accumulates offstage until it has grown into something very hard to face.

The Avoider usually doesn't meet trouble with panic or spiking anxiety (their in-the-moment regulation is fairly good), but the price of that calm is a steady loss of visibility. Holding the information at arm's length, they lose the chance to see what's coming. The way out runs through structures that keep working even when looking is hard: simple, automatic arrangements with few explicit choices, designed to shrink the effort it takes to stay

---

[6]Xavier Gabaix, "Behavioral Inattention," in Handbook of Behavioral Economics, ed. D. Bernheim, S. DellaVigna, and D. Laibson, vol. 2 (Elsevier, 2019), 261–343.

in control. The aim is a system that holds up even while your attention is somewhere else.

The Controller

The Controller doesn't control out of a love of command, or a love of order for its own sake. They control because uncertainty is hard to bear. Psychology has a name for the trait, intolerance of uncertainty: the tendency to meet anything that can't be fully pinned down with heightened vigilance and a hunger for foresight. That difficulty tolerating the unknown goes hand in hand with persistent anticipating and a search for security, even when the available control is limited.[7] In money, where some unpredictability is always present, the disposition feeds constant monitoring, less to improve the outcome than to dull the sense of vulnerability.

They're easy to spot. They live among spreadsheets, compare prices until the line between saving money and wasting time disappears, and audit each expense with the zeal of a prosecutor who suspects even himself. They log and they categorize, and none of it quite settles them, precisely because steady vigilance doesn't produce calm. When uncertainty climbs, the Controller speeds up. The more they check to reassure themselves, the further calm recedes, because the repetition keeps alive the very doubt it means to resolve. The Controller has the information and the good tools; what they have to learn is to trust systems that don't require their constant watch, which is especially hard for anyone who feels that the moment they look away, everything could turn to dust.

The Optimist

The Optimist doesn't deny that problems exist. They just rank them as minor, or at worst as part of a curve that's bound to straighten out. Their confidence is hard to erode: arguing them out

---

[7]R. Carleton, "Fear of the Unknown: One Fear to Rule Them All?," Journal of Anxiety Disorders 41 (2016): 5–21.

of it tends to be about as useful as talking someone out of their faith. The stubbornness has nothing to do with ignorance. An Optimist can know the figures cold, can even have lived through the consequences that ought to sharpen their read on a situation, and still hold a more powerful inner story alongside it, one in which past failures get recast as accidents, minor detours from a future that stays bright.[8] In the optimism bias, the brain steadily overrates the odds of success and underrates the odds of failure, above all when the wished-for outcome lines up with who we take ourselves to be, a tinted lens that colors perception and reasoning for good.

In money, that lens cuts both ways. On one side, it lets the Optimist move where others freeze, launching projects that would never exist if everyone weighed risk with surgical cool. On the other, it introduces a dangerous give into how they read limits. The Optimist always has something in motion, an opportunity that 'can't be passed up,' a venture that promises to make sense, in hindsight, of everything that came before.

This person tends to put off facing the numbers out of sheer confidence. There will be time to adjust; the cash flow will sort itself out. In the meantime they take on risk, sure that the intuition that has carried them through so often will carry them again. The catch is that intuition becomes the only criterion, which turns the decision into a bet. The Optimist is admirable for their initiative, for the knack of picturing scenarios no one else sees. Without people like this the world would be more predictable and a great deal poorer. The steady underrating of risk, and the ease of spending tomorrow's resources as if they were already in hand, is far less romantic. The Optimist isn't reckless, yet the confidence that tomorrow will clean up what today defers is its own hazard. Their dreams aren't the problem. A few soft brakes, the kind that add friction without stalling the engine, can do wonders, letting them keep building without mortgaging the future at every turn:

---

[8]T. Sharot, "The Optimism Bias," Current Biology 21 (2011): 941–945.

the goal is to keep the enthusiasm from burning down the very thing it meant to grow.

The Protector

If money had an explicit moral dimension, it would probably take the shape of the Protector, who experiences money as an instrument of care, less a medium of exchange than hard proof of emotional commitment. Helping and lending are the bricks of their private economy, and they outweigh any balance sheet. Emotional duty comes before financial duty, often without the person even realizing it. When someone close hits a problem, money shows up as a way to keep the other person from falling, even at the cost of the Protector's own footing.

Many Protectors grew up cast in a parent's role, learning to be 'the stable one' for the group before that should ever have fallen to them. Others settled into being the quiet support that always answers the call. In practice, this person lends money they don't have and covers debts that aren't theirs on the vague promise that 'it'll sort out later,' setting aside their own plans to put out fires they didn't start. Each gesture leaves a mix of relief at the rescue and wear from what it cost.

The Protector is built for generosity and care, though the rush to pay first and cover debts that aren't theirs runs alongside a need to feel necessary and central; money becomes the instrument of that position in a family or group. There's no point trying to make them selfish or drilling them on how to say 'no.' What helps is finding ways for their own wellbeing to count too, so that helping stops meaning the steady sacrifice of their own financial life. Once they see that getting themselves to safety betrays no one, self-care stops being a moral failure and becomes another form of love.

These profiles don't exhaust a person's economic identity, and they come nowhere near exhausting their identity as a whole. They are not fixed destinations either, but tools for naming the recurring dispositions that tend to fire in the face of uncertainty or loss. Such patterns can ease, even change, once they stop running implicitly and get recognized for what they are, because that recognition strips them of their automatic force.

For people with an avoidant or impulsive pattern, lectures change little; redesigning the context of the decision gets real results. Simple mechanisms, automatic enrollment in a savings plan with the option to leave, or contributions that step up gradually as raises come in, can shift behavior that looked immovable, because the financial signature is no longer the only force at the table. The pattern is still there, but it no longer governs on its own.

Knowing your own pattern, though, is necessary but not sufficient for reorienting your relationship with money. For a signature to stop organizing decisions, it has to be set inside a history that shows what once made it useful and what makes it costly now. Without that placement in time, every attempt at change falls apart. The move is from trait to trajectory, asking which reflexes fire, when they first appeared, what problem they originally solved, and why they stay active under conditions that have long since changed. Reconstructing the financial life line is central to exploring our identity on this terrain, and it gives any later transformation something solid to stand on. That is the work of the next section.

2. The Financial Life Line

“Financial life line” sounds like introspection or classic autobiography, and it's neither. The life line is a reading tool, a device that makes visible the regularities running through everyday experience in scattered, fragmentary form. Its aim is less to remember than to see better, so instead of reconstructing the past with precision, it reorganizes the past to bring implicit patterns to the surface. We aren't out to expose hidden truths or some single cause that explains everything. There probably isn't one. We're after recurring sequences linking situations, emotions, and decisions: which events trigger which responses, and which emotions and fixes show up again and again.

For the tool to work, you have to resist two common temptations. The first is to tidy the past so it "makes sense," smoothing over contradictions or justifying decisions after the fact. The second is the moral temptation to read your history as a ledger of rights and wrongs, virtues and flaws. Both distort the data and drain the exercise of its power. A reliable life line is honest in its mess, with no concern for coming out coherent or uplifting.

The focus belongs on the emotional experience attached to particular events, lifting the relevant ones out of their blur and making them observable. The line doesn't erase the patterns; it strips away their opacity, and that is the first step for any later work that depends on knowing what we're repeating and why. Here are the steps.

1. Draw the Line

The drawing is a deliberately simple way to put your own financial history onto a visible plane, with no preset hierarchy and no forced interpretation, free of anything technical or preparatory. Start by drawing a horizontal line and marking on it the memories that come up, not necessarily the most important ones in the abstract, but the ones that actually surface when you think about money in your life. As references pile up along the line, something shifts: money stops being a set of isolated figures and decisions and becomes a lived sequence, run through by the emotional states attached to different experiences. Noting how a particular moment felt (say, the mix of pride and fear around your first steady income) matters more than nailing down dates or amounts. What we're recording is the imprint left by events that still shape how we decide today.

It helps to jot down plain emotions: fear, excitement, relief, shame, uncertainty, pride. That emotional record is what behavioral psychology calls financial "metamemory," an internal archive that shapes what we do now even when we aren't conscious of it.

2. Look at It the Way You'd Look at a Map

Once the line is drawn, the next job is to look at it from enough distance that it stops feeling like a confession and starts working as something to be read. A gaze stripped of urgency lets regularities appear without your having to hunt for them. In that move, which turns your own experience into something almost foreign, you can start to notice how certain decisions tend to cluster in moments of pressure or relief. It's important to suspend all moral judgment and simply register how you responded and how that keeps operating now. That distance, more perceptual than analytic, opens a less defensive understanding of your relationship with money. Where are the spikes of anxiety, the places the "rush" factor repeats, and where does caution run to excess? Cognitive self-distancing improves decision-making because it turns off shame and turns on reflection.

3. Identify the Financial Signature

After walking the life line and stepping back from it, the challenge is to translate that material into a coherent reading. Identifying a financial signature means going past the description that flatters us most, or that fits the image we hold of ourselves, to detect which response shows up most consistently when money meets tension, fatigue, uncertainty, or expectation.

Watch which reaction fires before you can think too much, since the signatures express themselves as reflexes. Someone who recognizes themselves as an Accumulator will often notice that even when the numbers add up, the body doesn't relax: the relief is brief and functional, and right away the need returns to keep guarding, comparing, or postponing, as if stability were always provisional. Someone closer to the Compensator's logic, by contrast, will tend to spot the sequence of stretches of effort or depletion that end in a purchase felt as emotional relief, often followed by discomfort or a need to justify it. In both cases, the right signature is the one that accounts for what actually happens when discomfort arrives.

A common mistake is to confuse values with patterns. Many people believe they identify with a signature because they prize generosity or creativity, when the signature is really recognized by the cost it generates once it fires out of context. The Protector, for example, is identified by the repeated scenes where money goes to holding others up even when that means systematically setting aside one's own projects, leaving a persistent sense of depletion. The Controller is recognized by the difficulty of letting go without anxiety, even when the system is already working and needs no further intervention.

Pay attention to the justifications that show up after decisions. Each signature tends to carry a fairly stable internal story. The Optimist explains the present mismatches in the name of a future presented as imminent and restorative; the Avoider narrates the delay as a way of "not making things worse." Listening to that inner speech, what we tell ourselves to legitimize a decision, tends to be more revealing than the decision itself.

It's also worth remembering that a single pure signature rarely appears. In most cases there is a primary signature, which fires in stressful situations or major decisions, and a secondary one that emerges as a complementary or compensatory response. An Accumulator may turn to compensatory spending in moments of extreme exhaustion; a Protector may alternate stretches of support with phases of avoidance; a Controller may shift, at the breaking point, into briefly tuning out the numbers. Recognizing these combinations helps you avoid a simplistic label and makes better sense of the swings that appear along the line.

A good sign that you've got the identification right is that it brings no immediate relief. It opens instead onto a mix of clarity and discomfort, where something clicks without quite reassuring you. When the right signature appears, it usually disarms both the usual excuses and the excessive self-blame: not "this is wrong"; it says "this has a logic," one that made sense at another time.

Finally, let's remember it's important not to use the signature as a closed explanation. Above all, it serves to make clear that change runs through modifying the contexts and rules that keep the dominant pattern active. That's the work of the next step.

4. Name the Dominant Pattern

If the financial signature describes how we tend to respond when money comes into play, the dominant pattern identifies what triggers that response. This organizing principle sets a signature, or a combination of signatures, in motion over and over across our history. This step condenses the previous ones.

Looking at the line again, the new question is what gets activated before we decide. It may be a recurring emotion such as fear or urgency. It may be a context that tends to scramble judgment, like external uncertainty or the pressure of holding others up. It may be an implicit belief running through our history: the idea that there's never enough, say, or that the future will take care of what doesn't add up today. That's the level where the pattern operates.

An example helps show the difference. Two people may share a very similar signature (say, extreme caution and difficulty spending) and still be organized by different patterns. In one, the caution fires whenever there is a possibility of losing what has already been gained, so the pattern is tied to a fear of loss and a need to hold a known position. In the other, the same caution shows up when they feel they don't control the environment or that they depend on unpredictable external factors, so their pattern answers to a distrust of the context's stability rather than to loss itself. The behavior can look identical from outside, but the trigger is different, and so is the point of intervention.

Telling signature and pattern apart matters, because if we only recognize the signature, the later work turns generic, trying to "loosen up," "spend more," "control less," or "plan better," without touching whatever sets the response in motion. Once the pattern is clear, by contrast, we can move the focus to the right place and work on whatever pulls the trigger. The pattern marks the leverage point; the signature shows how that leverage turns into action.

This step closes the work with the life line, turning a narrative into a working hypothesis. The line shows what happened and how it felt. The signature names our habitual response. The pattern pinpoints the exact place that response fires from. From here we can leave the past in its place and put the priority on changing the present, without denying our history or forcing some supposed change of identity, simply altering the conditions that keep the pattern active.

3. The Myths That Hold the Patterns in Place

After identifying the life line, the financial signature, and the pattern that triggers it, one more layer of identity remains to examine. In that layer live the stories behind our repetitions. No pattern holds on emotion or habit alone. To persist over time it needs something that makes it look reasonable, even inevitable. These ideas rarely show up as explicit theories arrived at through reflection. They work more like condensed, seemingly obvious phrases, a "that's just how things are" that closes off the discomfort and lets us keep deciding with no inner friction.

These ideas we'll call financial myths. "Myth" might sound naive, or like an accusation of ignorance, but it's neither. Financial myths stabilize a way of relating to money. The myth makes economic reality emotionally livable, lowering the dissonance between what we feel, what we do, and what we say about ourselves.. Myths hold up remarkably well against contrary evidence, because they aren't there to be true.

These myths pass through household scenes, and tracking down their origin can be a fool's errand. They might be passing remarks, the tone of a family conversation, a parent's fear, a boss's exhaustion, repeated headlines, or long silences around the table. It doesn't matter. They are little homemade theories about how the economic world works, easy to remember and pass on, that settle in early and operate as default truths protecting the pattern that organizes them.

As long as the myth stays intact, the behavior looks natural and logical and shows no trace of emotional strategy. So once we've recognized how we react to money (the signature) and from which situations that reaction fires (the pattern), it becomes essential to dismantle the stories that make them unquestionable. Only when the myth loses its authority does the pattern stop running on automatic, and the chance to step out of the loop opens up. We won't list them all here, but reviewing some of the most common ones will sharpen the eye for the rest.

"Saving is for people who earn a lot"

This myth tends to show up strongly in lives marked by early scarcity or instability, and it works as a perfect alibi for patterns organized around caution or avoidance. If saving is something "other people" do, then there's nothing to examine in your own structure. The brain plays its part, favoring the immediate and discounting the distant, so setting money aside for an abstract future feels like an unjustified luxury.

In fact, as plenty of studies show, the capacity to save depends less on income level than on the way saving gets built into daily life. When saving demands sustained attention and willpower, it tends to fail even among people who earn well. When it leans instead on simple, low-cognitive-cost systems, it holds even in contexts of modest income and real instability.

International comparisons show that income level alone doesn't explain the differences in saving rates. Where structured mechanisms exist, from informal collective-saving arrangements to automated schemes, even low-income households manage to keep up consistent saving behavior. Saving, in that sense, is a system, and systems can be designed.[9]

"Managing money is complicated"

This myth tends to appear where one's own financial situation breeds discomfort, which makes it an efficient prop for patterns of avoidance or permanent delegation. When managing money is presented as an inherently complex task, the act of looking at the numbers stops registering as a navigational tool and becomes a source of threat. Not looking, in that context, comes to seem reasonable, since if something is too complicated, the sensible thing is to stay out of it.

But the real complexity isn't where this myth places it. There are corners of the economic world that are genuinely hard, like understanding sophisticated financial derivatives or modeling risk with advanced statistical tools. All of that takes specific training, but the day-to-day management of your own financial life isn't difficult on that order. What feels "complicated" is usually accumulated fatigue, shame at not knowing, or the overload of too many options that ends up paralyzing. When the alternatives multiply with no structure, the quality of decisions drops and the will to decide freezes. Clarity and simplicity in financial information, by contrast, lower anxiety and improve the capacity to act, even in people with no economic training. The problem, then, lies in the design of the decision environment.

The complexity myth freezes us, turning a learnable skill into an identity wall of the "this isn't for me" kind. Managing money requires neither genius nor technical virtuosity. We all do it, and

---

[9]See Abhijit V. Banerjee and Esther Duflo, Poor Economics: A Radical Rethinking of the Way to Fight Global Poverty (New York: PublicAffairs, 2011); Richard H. Thaler and Shlomo Benartzi, "Save More Tomorrow: Using Behavioral Economics to Increase Employee Saving," Journal of Political Economy 112.1 (2004): 164–187; and Sendhil Mullainathan and Eldar Shafir, Scarcity: Why Having Too Little Means So Much (New York: Times Books, 2013); together with the data in World Bank, World Development Report 2015: Mind, Society, and Behavior (Washington: World Bank, 2015).

we can do it better with simple systems that reduce the friction between information and action. By casting the everyday as unreachable, this myth defers that learning indefinitely.

"Investing is risky"

Put that way, the statement looks like an obvious truth expressing prudence, almost a responsible warning. Yet it hides a deep confusion about risk and where it comes from. Saying investing is risky is like saying driving a car is dangerous. The dangerous thing is doing it against the rules or without paying attention. Driving with your eyes closed is risky; driving with judgment isn't necessarily, or at most it carries dangers similar to plenty of other things we won't stop doing because they're the core of personal and social life. After all, the highest accident rate happens inside the home itself. How would we go about not living in a house, if everything came down to avoiding risk?

This myth, passing for good sense, ends up feeding patterns of extreme caution, where protecting the present becomes the priority even at the cost of the future. In that frame, any exposure to the market looks like a threat, while inaction gets experienced as neutral or safe. That neutrality is an illusion, because giving up investing doesn't eliminate risk. It just trades one kind for another, very specific and guaranteed one. Neuroeconomics shows that much of the fear tied to investing comes from the emotional experience of volatility. Watching a number rise and fall fires threat circuits even before any harm [10]materializes, making the screen more unsettling than the actual outcome. Meanwhile, less visible processes like inflation erode purchasing power steadily and silently, with a cumulative impact far greater than that of many one-off bad investment decisions.

[10]See Brian Knutson et al., "Anticipation of Increasing Monetary Reward Selectively Recruits Nucleus Accumbens," Journal of Neuroscience 21.16 (2001); and Brian Knutson et al., "Neural Antecedents of Financial Decisions," Neuron 58, no. 5 (2008): 814–822.

The risk myth, then, doesn't tell investing apart from improvising. Strategy gets confused with a gamble, horizon with impulse. We can say that investing with no information or no plan is genuinely risky, while investing on a sound design is, in essence, a way of managing time, setting resources to work today so they retain or grow their power to support tomorrow. In short, entering the market without tools is as risky as being shut out of it by fear, letting the passage of time work against us.

"Money can't buy happiness"

This line tends to come up when the conversation about money starts to chafe. It works nicely as a moral full stop that calms tensions and dodges hard questions. Saying money can't buy happiness lets us step back, claim a certain ethical high ground, and sidestep the question of what money actually does in daily life. In truth, money doesn't produce happiness in the full, existential sense of the word, but it does raise wellbeing up to a meaningful threshold, with no need for luxury or excess, by reducing uncertainty and exposure to threat. Covering an emergency, choosing without dread, living free of the constant weight of economic fragility. None of that makes anyone happy in any grand sense, yet it heads off many forms of everyday suffering, the kind that also make it impossible to be fully happy even if we're lucky enough to be handed existential happiness. Best not to ruin the perfection by neglecting the material.

When the distinction between full happiness and wellbeing gets erased, money slides into the place of an emotional substitute, and it has an astonishing capacity to do so. At that point the myth hides its flip side, where the use of money papers over emotional or relational gaps that map onto whatever each signature most needs. The Compensator looks for immediate relief; the Optimist for intensity and promise; the Protector for belonging through holding others up. In every case, money amplifies a demand that was already there. By flatly denying the link between money and happiness, the myth lets us use money as an emotional shortcut without taking on the cost of that move. If "money can't buy happiness," then there'd be nothing to examine in how it's spent, hoarded, lent, or avoided, because how it's used would have nothing to do with that. Dismantling this myth means giving money back its proper place: a tool for reducing uncertainty and widening options, not a substitute for emotional work. Seeing those cracks clearly, and the traps we set for ourselves, returns a certain lucidity, which in money matters is an unglamorous form of wellbeing.

"If I earn more, I'll be better off"

This myth is nearly universal and extraordinarily false. Consider the phenomenon of "hedonic adaptation" that governs our behavior. The term refers to our tendency to get used to changes quickly, including those that bring genuine pleasure or relief at first. The idea was formulated in psychology in the seventies, after researchers noticed that people tend to return, over time, to a relatively stable level of subjective wellbeing, even after events as intense as winning the lottery or suffering a serious loss.[11] The initial emotional impact fades, and what looked transformative gets folded into the new normal.

Out of this phenomenon came the popular metaphor of the hedonic treadmill, which captures how people can "run" after material improvements or higher income without actually moving forward in lasting wellbeing. Each new raise lifts satisfaction for a moment, then quickly becomes the new baseline, which in turn demands more to produce the same effect. The idea helps explain why improving external conditions, on its own, rarely solves the underlying financial problems. With no change in habits and decision patterns, more resources just feed the same story at a

[11] Philip Brickman and Donald T. Campbell, "Hedonic Relativism and Planning the Good Society," in Adaptation-Level Theory: A Symposium, ed. M. H. Appley (New York: Academic Press, 1971), 287–302; Philip Brickman, Dan Coates, and Ronnie Janoff-Bulman, "Lottery Winners and Accident Victims: Is Happiness Relative?," Journal of Personality and Social Psychology 36, no. 8 (1978): 917–927; and D. Kahneman, Thinking, Fast and Slow (New York: Farrar, Straus and Giroux, 2011).

larger scale, with more spending and more pressure. If that's how it works, a bigger income by itself won't leave us better off.

This myth tends to sustain patterns that put the deep work off indefinitely. If the improvement is always projected onto some future income, there's no urgency to examine the present, since today's decisions are justified in the name of a tomorrow that promises to make up for everything. Hedonic adaptation takes that promise apart with relentless logic: tomorrow arrives, but it arrives turned into today, and today, with no structural change, comes to feel insufficient again. Taking this myth apart lets us treat economic growth and subjective progress as related but distinct, each with its own logic, neither reducible to the other.

"Debt is bad"

Few phrases carry such an automatic moral charge. It's spoken with the same certainty as certain family truisms, as if debt were a failing in itself, a flaw of character or proof of irresponsibility. Yet debt, taken seriously, is neither good nor bad. It has no ethics of its own. What it has is a function, and like any tool, its effect depends on how it's used in a context, and above all on the motive that sets it in motion. Some debts work as bridges, letting you bring resources forward so you can produce or grow later on. Others cushion emergencies, head off momentary collapse, buy air when reality presses too hard. In those cases, debt is a reasonable answer to a concrete constraint. The trouble appears when debt stops connecting two moments and starts going in circles, sustaining a lifestyle you can't pay for, say, or covering tensions that find no other way out. Debt is a symptom, and we go wrong when we stare at an isolated number or lose ourselves in moral judgment. The symptom is telling us something that doesn't come from looking at the interest rate alone.

"I'm just not good with money"

This myth is probably the most damaging of all, because it goes beyond describing a particular difficulty and ends up declaring an identity. Saying "I'm not good with money" sounds humble and honest, when it actually hides a quiet shutdown that turns an acquirable skill into a fixed trait and blocks any real attempt at change. Once something becomes part of "who I am," it stops being ground to work on and turns into fate. A mistake then gets experienced as confirmation of identity, justifying an early retreat. Handling money is a cultural and practical skill, like cooking or public speaking. No one is born knowing how, and most people learn fairly fast once the costly noise of shame is switched off. As long as the difficulty registers as a personal defect, learning stays suspended. Recognize it as a trainable skill and the ground opens up. This myth has to be driven out with method and structure, dropping that inherited line that was never quite true.

Look at this small list of myths again. They're all functional to holding patterns in place, which is why when a myth weakens, the pattern loses its narrative backing and the signature stops governing. From here, the work shifts from understanding to design, building contexts and structures that let us decide differently without fighting ourselves.

* * *

When this chapter began, money could still look like a matter of figures and accounts. As the path went on, that appearance gave way, and we stopped looking for solutions in financial recipes to step into the relationship between money and our own history, made of habits taken on without deliberation, inherited fears, and patterns that once protected us but, over time, also began to hold us back. Once it becomes visible, that identity no longer rules us automatically. It leaves room for choice.

N

North

January. We sit down with a coffee and write in a fresh notebook: "This year I'm going to save, get out of debt, start investing, and stop wasting money on junk." We do it fast, with the clean energy of a fresh start, and for a while the list feels like a serious plan. By March, the notebook is in a drawer; by May, we don't remember which drawer. It's normal, really, to drop a goal here and there, but if the same ones come back every January, something is going on. That pattern is showing us something worth taking seriously, because part of us knows what it wants and can't manage to hold on to it. This step of the method is about understanding why this happens to us and building something that works differently.

Up to now the work has been backward-looking. We looked back to understand our relationship with money, made of primal scenes, automatic responses, and patterns still running on their own. Now let's look at direction. Planning means deciding, ahead of time, what kind of life we want to build, as if we can write part of your own story in advance. Seen that way, few things matter more. The most common mistake is to think financial planning is for tidy people, the kind who love a spreadsheet. Planning is really a narrative tool that answers the question of how we want our life to look a few years from now, and what our money has to do to make that possible. It's the question of what place money will take in future we imagine for ourselves. With no plan, money reacts to emergencies, putting out emergencies or sudden impulses. With a plan, money takes on distinct jobs. One part holds up the present, another works quietly to build a later. Money stops being a chaotic force and behaves like a coordinated system. Chapter N, for North, is about this, because our "future self" exists. The only question is whether it will meet an improvised life or one we took the trouble to plan.

1. The Brain That Won't Cooperate

Before we talk about goals, it's worth clearing up a few things about the machinery that will determine whether we meet them. Our brains are still ancient machines, built to survive the savanna rather than navigate online banking. That architecture still runs today, even though our decisions have left the hunt and the shelter behind for screens and deadlines. It is in that mismatch that cognitive biases emerge, patterns of perception and decision that hold deep regularities. Psychology began to study them systematically in the second half of the twentieth century, through cases where people decided badly in predictable ways. What looked irrational had, in fact, a very consistent internal logic.

One of those biases is what's called present bias, the tendency to give more weight to the immediate than to the distant. We sell it short if we see only raw impulsiveness or a lack of self-control, when this inherited sensitivity is a window onto the oldest human history, a time when putting off a reward could mean losing it. Picture a Homo sapiens in East Africa, in the Rift Valley region of present-day Kenya, toward the end of the late Pleistocene, some 40,000 years ago. He lives in a nomadic band, with no agriculture and no way to store food for long, dependent on resources that come and go: seasonal fruit, small animals, occasionally scavenged carrion. When he finds ripe fruit, eating it right away secures energy in a setting where the next chance is uncertain. Keeping some for later carries concrete risks: it may spoil within hours in the heat, or other band members may claim it. Hiding it is no better, since a forced move could keep him from coming back to the same spot. In that environment, favoring the immediate was an adaptive strategy against the unreliability of the food supply. That same mechanism, carried into the present, makes the decisions that promise fast relief especially attractive, even when the bill eventually comes due. The brain, which doesn't tell danger apart from discomfort, answers both with urgency.

Another frequent move is optimistic projection, a persistent leaning toward imagining the future as more orderly and more generous than the present. Next month always looks lighter, the next paycheck easier to handle, with the future version of yourself reliably more disciplined than the current one. This illusion usually isn't experienced as self-deception but as a reasonable expectation, and it works as a soothing story that lets us put off uncomfortable adjustments under the implicit promise that things will be different later on.

Loss aversion is more emotional. Losses carry a bigger psychological impact than gains, even when the amounts are equal. So our decisions don't aim so much at maximizing gains as at avoiding losses.[12] In a famous experiment at Duke University, where basketball is a religion and tickets are so scarce they're handed out by lottery after students camp for days outside the arena, researchers phoned students who had won tickets and students who hadn't, asking the winners how much they would sell theirs for and the others how much they would pay to get one.[13] Strikingly, those without a ticket offered to pay, on average, about 170 dollars; those who had won wouldn't let go for less than 2,400. The same ticket, obtained the same way, was worth fourteen times

---

[12]See Daniel Kahneman and Amos Tversky, "Prospect Theory: An Analysis of Decision under Risk," Econometrica 47, no. 2 (1979): 263–291; Nicholas C. Barberis, "Thirty Years of Prospect Theory in Economics: A Review and Assessment," Journal of Economic Perspectives 27, no. 1 (2013): 173–196.

[13]Ziv Carmon and Dan Ariely, "Focusing on the Forgone: How Value Can Appear So Different to Buyers and Sellers," Journal of Consumer Research 27 (2000): 360–370.

more to the person already holding it, simply because parting with it felt like a loss. The everyday version happens to anyone putting their car up for sale. The owner folds the years they've lived into the price and asks well above what the market will pay, because to them selling cheap means losing something of their own; the buyer just sees a car. In the end the overpriced car sits unsold for months, and the owner, stubborn but also fed up, comes to believe selling is hard and closes a terrible deal for less than they'd have gotten with a realistic price from the start. Loss aversion ends up causing the loss.

The sunk-cost fallacy describes the difficulty of abandoning something we've already poured a lot into, even when it's stopped making sense. A sunk cost is what we've already spent and won't get back no matter what, which is exactly why it should be irrelevant to deciding what to do from here on. But it isn't, because quitting feels like admitting that everything put in before was for nothing. The most famous case, enough to give the bias another name, is the Concorde. When the French and British governments already knew the supersonic jet would never turn a profit, they kept investing for years, because stopping something they had put so much into seemed an unbearable waste.[14] They built barely two dozen planes, never recovered what they'd spent, and retired the aircraft in 2003. The people deciding were sophisticated officials with every analysis on the table, which shows that knowing the bias exists doesn't make us immune to it.

We do the same thing constantly. Think of that boring movie we keep watching because we already paid for the ticket, as if staying in the seat could recover the money. Or the course that bores us but whose full fee we already paid, the washing machine we keep repairing because we've already spent a fortune on it, the investment going under that we can't bring ourselves to exit. The truth is that past money is already gone. Instead of staying

---

[14]Hal R. Arkes and Catherine Blumer, "The Psychology of Sunk Cost," Organizational Behavior and Human Decision Processes 35, no. 1 (1985): 124–140.

prisoners of how much went into something, we can ask whether, starting from zero today and with what we now know, we would put money there again. That almost always breaks the spell.

Very quietly, the status quo effect leads us to leave things as they are even when it doesn't serve us. Here the drag isn't a calculation about sunk costs. It’s the sense that changing takes energy and risks a mistake, while doing nothing looks effortless. Between the concrete discomfort of acting today and the diffuse discomfort of a chronic malfunction, the brain almost always picks the second, because it doesn't feel like a decision. And so we spend years with the same expensive bank account even when better options exist. It's not that we think it's fine: opening the matter, comparing options, and taking the step feels more expensive than living with the problem. The priciest version is the budget we never chose. Huge numbers of people spend month after month on a pattern they never deliberately decided. It simply formed on its own, through accumulated habit, and keeps going by inertia. The status quo quietly turns choices into destiny. The good news is that the same mechanism can work in our favor once we invert the start. Getting a change going is hard, but once it's installed, the inertia that used to hold the bad in place starts holding the good, for instance when we automate healthy financial decisions so that laziness, which is unavoidable, works on our side instead of against us.

There's another cross-cutting mechanism that explains many everyday inconsistencies in how we deal with money. Richard Thaler called it mental accounting: the tendency to divide money into sealed mental compartments, each with its own rules.[15] We can guard the same amount with extreme care or spend it lightly depending on the label we've given it. We feel an “extra” bit of

---

[15] Richard H. Thaler, "Mental Accounting and Consumer Choice," Marketing Science 4, no. 3 (1985): 199–214. See also Drazen Prelec and George Loewenstein, "The Red and the Black: Mental Accounting of Savings and Debt," Marketing Science 17, no. 1 (1998): 4–28; and I. Kamalini et al., "The Effect of Financial Literacy, Mental Accounting, and Risk Aversion on Students' Investment Decisions," International Journal of Economics, Management and Accounting 2, no. 4 (2025): 158–170.

income, for instance, as something we can make disappear right away, even when our overall situation is fragile. Formally there's no difference between amounts, but we live and use them differently.

In a famous experiment, one group was given the scene of buying a theater ticket for ten dollars that then gets lost. Would they buy another? In the second scenario, the ticket costs ten dollars but on arriving at the box office the person realizes they've lost a ten-dollar bill and faces the same question. In both situations ten dollars are missing, but the answers came out opposite. With the lost ticket, only 46 percent said they'd buy another; with the lost bill, 88 percent bought the ticket without a problem.[16] Why? In the first case the mind charges the lost ten dollars to the "theater account," and buying another ticket makes it feel like the outing cost twenty, which seems like too much. In the second, the lost bill belongs to the mental "cash" account and doesn't contaminate the cost of the show.

Mental accounting lets us save in one account and borrow in another without any clear sense of contradiction, because our minds treat them as entirely separate situations. A budget that imposes a logic ignoring this often fails, and loses the chance to use the mechanism as an ally. The "mental accounts" that separate rent money from vacation money, or the savings envelope from day-to-day spending, make a budget manageable, but you have to keep them in view.

When we cross these biases with the financial signatures we explored in I, we see that each one's traits get reinforced. For the Compensator, present bias brings immediate relief at an intensity the future can't match. In the Accumulator, loss aversion turns any expense into a small threat. When the Avoider thinks about changing, looking at the numbers produces a discomfort the brain reads as danger, and off they run, while the status quo offers them

---

[16]Daniel Kahneman and Amos Tversky, "The Framing of Decisions and the Psychology of Choice," Science 211, no. 4481 (1981): 453–458.

deep comfort. The Protector takes the sunk-cost fallacy to heart and keeps putting resources into others because they've already put in too much, and quitting would feel like a loss of centrality after so much sacrifice. These biases don't disappear with good intentions, but we can design goals that account for them from the start and make everyday heroism unnecessary.

2. The Goal Portfolio

Traditional personal-finance books ask us to do everything at once. Save, invest, get out of debt, build an emergency fund, think about retirement, study more, and don't forget to start a business. It all comes together and it's all urgent. The result is guilt and paralysis, which blocks any meaningful change. Let's leave that behind and make an INVERSO turn. Instead of piling up disconnected objectives, we'll build a goal portfolio to organize us, knowing that not all investments serve the same function or operate on the same time horizon.

The central criterion for building that portfolio is distance. The short term (3 to 6 months) gathers goals aimed at stabilizing your current life: easing the squeeze, creating a minimal margin to maneuver. The medium term (1 to 2 years) groups goals meant to produce visible change: a new income source, a completed course of study. The long term (3 to 5 years or more) holds goals that change your identity. They might be professional pivots, a move, or maybe the plan for your old age.

People whose objectives conflict with one another make less progress and feel worse, because they set many desires competing for the same mental resources with no priority criterion.[17] When "get out of debt," "travel," and "save for an apartment" all sit on

[17]R. A. Emmons and L. A. King, "Conflict Among Personal Strivings: Immediate and Long-Term Implications for Psychological and Physical Well-Being," Journal of Personality and Social Psychology 54, no. 6 (1988): 1040–1048.

the same time plane, each expense becomes a small betrayal of the other goals.

The brain also processes the near and the far differently. Short-term goals take concrete form; long-term ones activate deeper motivations.[18] Mix the two registers in the same list and the brain tries to run in two modes at once. Place each goal on its own horizon and it operates in the register that fits it. A mental trick that works well is to build a portfolio with different horizons where the goals cooperate. A short-term goal can emotionally support a long-term one ("this month I managed to save what I planned, and that brings me closer to something that matters"), and a medium-term goal can light up the meaning of the daily effort ("I'm finishing a degree that in a year could change my income"). Each one speaks to a different part of the mind.

But there are no tricks for everything. It's best to accept from the outset that only a few of the things we want can be carried out well at the same time. We can keep at most three financial goals active, one per time horizon. We don't have to discard the rest, but we can park it on a waiting list with no claim on constant attention. This limit keeps our ambition in check so it doesn't eat up mental energy.

Let's add a distinction that ruins most January notebooks: not all goals are alike. Outcome goals describe what we want to see at the end of the road: an amount saved, a debt brought down. They work as appealing images of the after. Process goals describe what we do regularly, whether or not we feel like it, whether or not the real world is bent on wrecking our plans. They're repeated behaviors, deeply unglamorous, that end up tipping the balance, because they're the ones that transform things. The first kind are like those spectacular trailers that turn out to front a forgettable film, all explosions and no plot. Process goals are the good screenwriter's gem: the ones that build a solid story. If we have

[18]On Construal-Level Theory, see Y. Trope and N. Liberman, "Construal-Level Theory of Psychological Distance," Psychological Review 117, no. 2 (2010): 440–463.

only outcome goals, then every time the real world picks on us (and it does so with admirable dedication), we'll feel like failures. Planning gets serious when we understand that it's all about doing it bit by bit.

Identity goals are the third kind: they aim at who we want to be in relation to money. Those future versions of ourselves order our present decisions, like reaching a comfortable footing, or not needing to borrow to soothe a bad day. Unlike traditional goals, they don't break when a month goes badly, because they mark a sustained direction. Held clearly, they keep us company and let even the stumbles become part of the road rather than catastrophic failures.

The planning this chapter proposes works as an articulated system. To choose goals without self-deception, it helps to start with no filters, writing down everything that shows up as a desire, with no ranking. "Get out of debt," "buy an apartment," "travel," "work less," "study something new," "start a business," "save," "sleep easy." Everything goes in. We begin by choosing one goal of deep meaning for the long term, and with our eye on it we choose another important one aimed at visible change for the medium term, doable in a year or two, and an urgent goal to stabilize the present, to be met in the short term (3 to 6 months). Everything else stays there, waiting. The question is how to choose them well.

3. Anatomy of a Goal That Survives

We won't use the usual methods. It's worth saying so outright, because more than one alert reader might be expecting to find them here. After all, SWOT (strengths, weaknesses, opportunities, and threats) is the classic tool whenever planning comes up. It's taught in universities, it shows up in management handbooks, and it slips, almost by inertia, into many self-help books that try to "organize your life" with the same logic you'd use to organize a company. It's a very effective tool for organizations making collective decisions, but we aren't companies, and we don't hold our decisions free of conflict.

Let's look at other tools through Ana's case. She's 38, works as a freelance designer, so her income swings, and she's just decided she needs to build an emergency fund. That's reasonable. Let's see what happens when she tries to build the goal.

The first thing Ana needs is clarity. Behavioral psychology offers a set of criteria for that, known as SMART (specific, measurable, achievable, relevant, time-bound), repeated so often they've lost their force.[19] They're no magic recipe, but they do force desires down to earth. "I want to improve my finances" means nothing; "I want to save $500 a month for 24 months to build a $12,000 emergency fund" is specific enough that the brain can follow it without getting confused. Ana frames her goal this way. It's measurable, time-bound, achievable without wrecking her life, and directly relevant: as a freelancer, every slow-paying client upends everything. So far so good, but clarity doesn't protect her from quitting. When a project falls through in April and she has a lean month, the transfer to the savings account gets suspended. One month turns into two, and by June she no longer remembers which month she stopped. Reality killed the goal, and there was no mechanism in place to prevent it.

That's where a second tool comes in, WOOP (wish, outcome, obstacle, plan), which starts from a simple idea. Beyond knowing what we want, we have to anticipate what will get in the way of reaching it. Instead of losing ourselves dreaming up the perfect future, we think about where the plan might break.[20] Ana applies

---

[19] George T. Doran, "There's a S.M.A.R.T. Way to Write Management's Goals and Objectives," Management Review 70, no. 11 (1981): 35–36. See also Edwin A. Locke and Gary P. Latham, "Building a Practically Useful Theory of Goal Setting and Task Motivation," American Psychologist 57, no. 9 (2002): 705–717.

[20] Gabriele Oettingen, Rethinking Positive Thinking: Inside the New Science of Motivation (New York: Current, 2014).

it. Her wish is to live with less stress, the outcome she's after is having an emergency fund, the obstacle is that in lean months the temptation to pause saving is enormous, and for that she designs a conditional plan: "If I earn less than usual in a given month, instead of suspending the transfer I cut it in half." It's better than nothing, because it anticipates the sabotage, but it still depends on Ana, in a month of financial stress, executing a decision that takes self-control exactly when she's most depleted.

A third tool, implementation intentions, attacks this flank by moving the decision into the past. It defines which action happens in response to which trigger and at what moment: "When X happens, I'll do Y," with surgical precision.[21] Ana adjusts: "On the 1st of each month, at 8 a.m., I review my income and make the transfer to the fund before paying anything else." When the behavior is tied to a concrete situation, we carry it out with almost no deliberation.

Ana's goal now has clarity, behavioral realism, and an automated trigger. For six months she keeps it up with real effort. The system seems to work, but in the seventh month it breaks. What happened? The thing to know is that Ana is a Compensator. That doesn't make her irresponsible. When stress piles up, her brain seeks immediate relief with a force that no statement of intent can counter. In bad months, present bias wins, and July was a bad month. A big project got complicated, a client owes her two invoices, and the washing machine stopped working. When August 1st arrives Ana is exhausted; she makes the transfer to the fund as planned, but she's forgotten that the insurance debit moved dates, and a negative balance with a fee shows up. She fixes it by hand, irritated.

The following weekend, after another hard week, she treats herself to something that wasn't in the budget. It's not much, but mental accounting has already done its work, convincing her the

---

[21] Peter M. Gollwitzer, "Implementation Intentions: Strong Effects of Simple Plans," American Psychologist 54, no. 7 (1999): 493–503.

treat comes out of a different "little box" than savings, so she doesn't feel it as a contradiction. The automatic transfer is still set up, but Ana suspends it "just this month" because income was lower. By September the fund has gone two months with no contributions and she hasn't even noticed, because nothing alerts her. Meanwhile, what she'd already built up sits in the same account where the rest of her money moves, so when she needs to organize her birthday in October, she uses all of it without thinking too hard. After all, "I'll just put it back." The fund, a separate entity in her head, was never separate in the architecture of her financial life.

What went wrong? Her tools never checked whether the goal was compatible with Ana's financial signature. A Compensator under stress needs the system to keep her from undoing the goal in the moment of vulnerability. The August suspension was present bias operating as it always does, this time with the pause button a click away. The big October birthday was a predictable consequence, because the money was operationally available in the checking account. The months without contributions were fed by the absence of any mechanism to stop the interruption before it became the new status quo.

Even if Ana weren't a Compensator, the scheme was just as fragile. If she were an Avoider, she'd simply have stopped dealing with it. If she were an Optimist, she'd have redirected part of the fund into "an opportunity I can't pass up." The signature changes, the failure mechanism changes, but the blind spot is the same. All three tools model goals in isolation, without assessing the behavioral and operational system those goals have to work inside. As we'll see in E, consistency over time is the basic mechanism of compounding returns, so this matters a great deal.

This is where the INVERSO Method adds an extra layer, making the goal compatible with the financial signature and the architecture of the system. ARCO goes further: its four dimensions, Anchoring (to identity), Realism (operational),

Counter-sabotage (structural), and Orchestration (systemic), protect the goal so it survives off the page.

Let's start with Anchoring. This diagnostic phase crosses two variables: our concrete goal, which we can sharpen with the SMART criteria, and our financial signature, paying attention to the predictable interference pattern, the specific way our behavioral bias will try to steer the goal off course until it's drained of function. Three questions help locate it.

First: what do I find easiest and hardest about this goal? The easy part tends to line up with the signature (the Accumulator saves effortlessly, the Controller organizes without being asked) and the hard part sits in tension with it. The goal breaks at the point of tension, when it asks something hard of us.

Second: when does my signature fire most strongly? The moments in a goal's cycle differ. The Optimist is most vulnerable when the goal is going well and the fund builds up a tempting sum; the Avoider wobbles at the moment of review and oversight. Spotting the when of the risk is as important as spotting the what, so we can be ready.

Third: which distorted version of the goal would feel most comfortable to me? Sabotage usually shows up as reinterpretation. The Optimist redirects toward "something better"; the Protector "helps for good reasons." If we can anticipate the distorted version, we can design something against it. Anchoring doesn't solve these problems yet, but it names them precisely enough for the next layers of ARCO to act. The first thing ARCO recognizes is that the main risk factor is inside us.

The second element is Realism, whose job is to gauge whether our goal can hold up under the real conditions we live in. The answer is never a quick yes or no, because motivation and the capacity to decide are variable, which is why we need a built-in margin of error that absorbs the instability without breaking continuity. Sometimes a single month of falling short generates a psychological cost out of all proportion to its real financial impact, because it becomes proof that we can't do it. With a margin of error, we don't give up so fast.

The margin of error works with three concrete parameters. The first is an operating range with a floor and a ceiling: the floor is the minimum we can keep up even in a terrible month; the ceiling is the most we can contribute in an exceptional one without throwing our life into chaos. The second is the automatic-adjustment rule, by which the amount varies without requiring deliberation. For example, if income falls more than a defined percentage below the three-month average, the contribution drops to the floor. If it rises above the average by a defined percentage, it climbs to the ceiling. The exact percentages depend on the case, but what matters is that the rule exists before the need arises. The third is the success criterion. The goal isn't measured by continuity alone. Twenty-four straight months contributing within the range, even if some months are at the floor, is a resounding success.

Twelve months at the ceiling followed by twelve months of abandonment is a failure, however equal or greater the total accumulated. Ana can reframe with this logic: "I'll save between $400 and $600 a month by automatic transfer on the 7th of each month, after confirming the fixed payments went through. If my income in a given month falls more than 20 percent below the three-month average, I drop the floor to $300 that month. If things go very well and my income beats the average by more than 30 percent, I raise the ceiling to $750. My aim is to keep continuity for 24 months."

The third element is structural Counter-sabotage, the shield for our goals. Anchoring diagnosed the pattern threatening the goal. Realism calibrated margins so the goal won't break under real variability. And what if the dominant bias fires anyway? Suppose Ana had another terrible week. This time a client demanded three rounds of changes that weren't in the budget, another canceled a project, and the washing machine broke again. She's exhausted. Out of nowhere an ad pops up on her phone for a handbag in the color she loves. It's expensive, but her hand drifts toward the click.

WOOP says "if I'm about to spend out of tiredness, I wait 10 minutes," but waiting those 10 minutes demands exactly the cognitive resource that's most depleted right then.

Structural Counter-sabotage brings in a logic that redesigns the environment so the obstacle has nowhere to operate.[22] The choice of measures depends on three parameters. First, the nature of the risk. Does the bias work by action or by omission? Risks of action (spending, diverting funds, overinvesting) call for measures that introduce friction, delays or costs between the impulse and its execution. Risks of omission, like not reviewing, instead need friction removed, automating the behavior.

Second, the intensity of the vulnerable moment. Moderate, recurring impulses, like Friday's takeout, are neutralized with permanent restrictions, like liquidity limits and accounts with no card attached. High-intensity impulses, the kind that come with the euphoria of a bull market or a relative's plea in a crisis, demand predefined, non-negotiable quantitative rules set before the moment of pressure, because when intensity rises, the capacity to deliberate drops.

Third, the relational cost of the measure. Some protections operate in solitude (setting up an account, establishing an automatic debit) while others involve other people: saying no to a request for help, negotiating spending limits with a partner. Measures that create relational conflict have to lower the emotional load of the decision, offering legitimate responses that reduce the confrontation. Saying "I won't lend you the money" isn't the same as "all my money is committed to fixed expenses this month." Refusing a couple's expense flat out isn't the same as pointing to a prior agreement. One response appeals to willpower, which falters precisely under pressure; the other appeals to an external, agreed-upon rule that depersonalizes the refusal and makes it far easier to hold. Turning a personal "no" into "that's

---

22Richard H. Thaler and Cass R. Sunstein, Nudge: Improving Decisions about Health, Wealth, and Happiness (New Haven: Yale University Press, 2008).

how my system works" takes the conflict out of the territory of affection and moves it to the territory of rules, where it hurts less and holds up better.

Back to Ana. As a Compensator, she's exposed to risk by action (spending), of moderate but frequent intensity and with no relational cost (the decision happens in solitude, in front of a screen). What she needs is for the savings money to be inaccessible for everyday spending (compensatory spending loses force when there's friction) and for discretionary spending to carry a predefined ceiling that doesn't depend on real-time decisions. If she has room within that ceiling, Ana can buy herself a handbag or order takeout without guilt, but once the cap is hit, that's it. Counter-sabotage defines what has to happen.

If Ana were an Optimist, the counter-sabotage would be completely different, because her goals would be threatened by irresistible investments. The risk by action, high-intensity and infrequent, needs strong friction, for example a certificate of deposit that only releases on an agreed date, along with rules that can't be reinterpreted, since reinterpretation is this profile's favorite form of sabotage. If Ana were an Avoider, the counter-sabotage would flip entirely: the risk is omission: a silent drip of postponements that pile up until the goal dies. She'd need an automatic-debit system with a predefined range, no manual intervention, a savings account with no everyday access, and a passive alert that fires only when something falls outside the acceptable range. The goal would survive because the system would move forward without Ana holding it up. Three signatures, the same goal, three completely different designs.

The fourth criterion is systemic Orchestration. A goal can be well designed, well diagnosed, and equipped with protection specs, yet badly fitted into its environment. If it sits in a tangle where the payment calendar, account structure, budget flow, and review mechanisms collide, the goal is doomed. ARCO's orchestration keeps that from happening. For this it takes the specs produced by Counter-sabotage and implements five measures.

Through functional separation, money that serves different functions goes in different places, because when two functions share the same space, the more urgent one always devours the more important one. Orchestration works out the how: whether to have one account for operations and fixed debits, one for the emergency fund with no card attached, one card for discretionary spending with a weekly limit, and eventually an investment account for when the overall plan takes off. Everything has an assigned address before we touch it.

Taking the time sequence into account, each financial move takes a place on the calendar that doesn't collide with the others. If saving competes on the same date with the fixed debits, it'll lose. Orchestration groups all the fixed payments, say between the 3rd and the 5th of the month, places the automatic transfer to the emergency fund on the 7th, after confirming the debits went through without incident, and loads the weekly discretionary spending on Mondays. Each move happens after the previous one is complete, eliminating the collisions.

Applying the budget hierarchy, we set the order in which income gets allocated the moment it comes in. That order decides what survives when the month gets hard. For this, once again, we have to flip the usual sequence. Most people spend first and hope to save whatever's left, but at the end there's nothing left, because expenses swallow all available income. The budget hierarchy reverses that order: the moment the money comes in, it sets the savings aside and leaves the rest available for everyday spending. That way, saving is a done deal that happened first. Back to Ana, the budget hierarchy is what guarantees she doesn't have to decide month to month how much to save. Saving comes to depend on structure, which is far more reliable than discipline.

Periodic visibility lets us monitor what's necessary, with a review frequency and format suited to each profile. We'll come back to this, but for now let's just say that someone prone to over-monitoring is better off with a spaced-out, brief review, so as not to feed the obsession, while someone who tends to avoid does better with a more frequent, very simple review, almost a glance, so that avoidance doesn't pile up surprises. The review exists to catch small deviations in time, while they're still easy to correct and before they turn into a problem.

The fifth component is transitional continuity, which handles the moment a goal is met. When we reach the objective, the habit that sustained it has no destination and risks dissolving. Rebuilding it later, from scratch, costs far more than having kept it running. So orchestration plans the transition in advance. For instance, the monthly automatic transfer gets redirected toward the investment account with no manual reconfiguration. The system preserves the continuity of the habit just by changing the destination.

Let's see it all together in Ana's case. Counter-sabotage specified that savings must be inaccessible and discretionary spending must have a ceiling that doesn't depend on real-time decisions. Orchestration implements it like this: the day the income arrives, the system distributes it automatically. The fixed payments run between the 3rd and the 5th. On the 7th, with the debits confirmed, the transfer to the emergency fund runs automatically within the range calibrated by Realism. What's left is split between the month's operating reserve and discretionary spending, which goes on a card with a weekly cap. Each quarter, a notification shows progress and projection. If the average contribution drops below the threshold, an alert fires. When the fund is full, the flow redirects straight to investing. In this operating architecture, each component takes a spec from Counter-sabotage and gives it a place, a time, and a mechanism. The goal stops being a task we have to remember and becomes something the system does while we get on with the rest of our lives.

What have we achieved with this? A solid goal in the INVERSO Method satisfies six criteria at once. It has the formal clarity of SMART, the friction-anticipation of WOOP, and the behavioral automation of implementation intentions, but ARCO adds, on top of that, identity Anchoring (A), which diagnoses the dominant bias threatening the goal; operational Realism (R), which calibrates margins for real conditions; structural Counter-sabotage (C), which specifies the conditions the environment must meet to neutralize the bias; and Orchestration (O), which implements those conditions in a sustainable financial architecture. The first three are necessary but not sufficient; the second three turn a formally correct goal into a successful one.

* * *

Defining a north introduces direction. How do we now get our actions to line up with it? We can know what we want and still be lost, because we're missing information about what's actually happening. Our daily decisions and our goal design unfold inside a system we rarely see in full. Income, expenses, old commitments, and small leaks pile up without our fully understanding how they interact. If that's so, there's no way our goal design fits our concrete reality. Before a north can guide us, it hast to connect with the reality of our financial lives. For that, the method requires making the financial structure around us visible.

V

Visibility

When we don't pay attention, our financial life behaves like a stray cat: elusive, unpredictable, and always returning at the end of the month with a torn ear and a story that's hard to follow. How many times have we dodged precise accounting and told ourselves we spend very little, only to end up praying next month will be better with no idea how we got here? That kind of self-deception is expensive. In the INVERSO Method, Visibility is central, but we won't rush straight into spreadsheets and expense tracking. Let's turn the question upside down again. What matters is not how much we spend but the kind of life we want to sustain. So we'll look first at how we earn our living, and then at what we can do with it.

1. The Architecture of Income

Work is far more than a way to get money. It regulates our days, gives us a place in the community, and shapes many of our personal aims. Pull on this thread and it leads far: toward vocation, family, and each person's place in society. When what we do is broadly aligned with what we enjoy, and the effort we put in with the reward we get, an important part of our life is in balance. When that alignment is missing, no budget solves the underlying problem.

That's why the INVERSO Method asks what kind of life we want to live and what income architecture can sustain it. The answer isn't universal, because there's no single way of working that's best for everyone. Insisting on that kind of formula usually ends with the uncomfortable realization that something doesn't fit. We can spend years earning good money while sacrificing time for things that mattered more, securing stability at the cost of our own unhappiness. Looking clearly at your own source of income is how you tell whether the way you earn money sustains the life you want or sabotages it.

There are three basic ways of relating to work, each calling for a different income architecture. For some, work is a means to fund something else. Raising children, pursuing hobbies, traveling, resting, whatever it may be. Someone who lives this way needs predictable income and low volatility, because they want a clear boundary between work and private life. They have few growth expectations, because they'd rather put in the minimum work that yields what they need to live the way they want. The stable employee with fixed hours who earns just enough and pours their free time into their kids is the typical example. There's nothing resigned about it. They simply chose where to put their life's center of gravity.

For others, work is a central part of identity. Here vocation comes first, and as long as the task points at what matters and brings in enough income, it's experienced as good, even if it pays less than other lines of work. This path usually means a long horizon of modest earnings in exchange for building something worthwhile, plus a high tolerance for irregular months, because meaning weighs more than salary.[23] The researcher who'd rather

[23]On the first two archetypes, see Amy Wrzesniewski, Clark McCauley, Paul Rozin, and Barry Schwartz, "Jobs, Careers, and Callings: People's Relations to Their Work," Journal of Research in Personality 31, no. 1 (1997): 21–33.

take a limited grant on a project they're passionate about than an administrative job paying twice as much embodies this profile. "Follow your passion" sounds very romantic, though it can be tricky advice. Passion often arrives after you get good at something, not before, and those who seem to be sailing on the sweet waters of vocation can end up more bored or frustrated than someone who starts purely for the salary and discovers a creative vein that leaves them fulfilled.

For others, finally, work is an investment in the future, tied to accumulating skills, contacts, and capital that multiply options. This means a deliberate sacrifice in the present, earning less today on a bet to earn more later, like the junior who accepts a lower salary at a startup where they learn ten times faster than at a corporation.[24]

These three models are connected. The same person moves among them depending on the moment of life. They may be in transition or combine elements of several at once. What they can't do, without paying dearly, is operate by the logic of one while building the architecture of another. Seeking stability and free time while assembling a structure that demands volatility and a massive investment of hours, for instance, will blow up sooner or later. The mismatch usually comes from a sloppy choice. We take and keep jobs without asking whether they sustain the life we want; we embrace a calling without working out whether it pays for itself; we invest in a future without setting deadlines or success criteria. Seeing which one we're standing in, and whether the architecture is consistent, is the first task of visibility over income.

Once we've done this, it's worth examining the source through five lenses that bring it into focus.

---

[24]Nassim Nicholas Taleb, Antifragile: Things That Gain from Disorder (New York: Random House, 2012); and Cal Newport, So Good They Can't Ignore You: Why Skills Trump Passion in the Quest for Work You Love (New York: Grand Central Publishing, 2012).

The first is substitutability. How much of what we do could a machine do? On what timeline?[25] Until not so long ago, income was a relatively stable variable that ran in a straight line: more education led to more work, a higher salary, and steady progress. That sequence broke. Digitization decoupled work from physical place, and artificial intelligence is doing the same with work and skills, altering the relationship between value and effort at a frantic pace. At the rate we're going, the window is measured in quarters. Expertise once protected by years of training is wobbling, and it's dragging "routinizable" complex work down with it. The most recent analyses of the impact of large language models show that the frontier no longer advances only on routine manual work; it's moving onto skilled intellectual work that was thought to be armored.[26] Junior programming, which two years ago looked like a safe career, is collapsing: one senior with an AI now does the work of five beginners. Plenty of people predict that the future belongs to the plumber or the electrician, since someone has to run cable, cool the racks, and keep the physical world running, at least until the robots arrive.

In truth, the catastrophist narrative is fairly useless. Automation doesn't advance evenly. It reaches some sectors before others, depends on geography and company size, runs into integration costs almost no one calculates, and consistently underestimates the emergence of new tasks, as in every technological revolution. Every limit of the machine is an area of opportunity that didn't exist before.

Visibility requires us to ask what we're doing today so that when it arrives it doesn't find us paralyzed, whether we use AI to defend our position or get displaced by someone who does. The answer changes with the type of work. If we use work as a means, high

---

[25] Carl Benedikt Frey and Michael A. Osborne, "The Future of Employment: How Susceptible Are Jobs to Computerisation?," Technological Forecasting and Social Change 114 (2017): 254–280.

[26] Tyna Eloundou, Sam Manning, Pamela Mishkin, and Daniel Rock, "GPTs Are GPTs: An Early Look at the Labor Market Impact Potential of Large Language Models," arXiv preprint arXiv:2303.10130 (2023).

substitutability strikes right at our priority of stability. If vocation is in play, it's possible, though not certain, that the loss of routine tasks becomes a chance to shed bureaucracy. If we're aiming at the future with skills in a substitutable zone, our investment is doubtful and we should redirect our efforts. In any case, ignoring the change or betting solely on long, generic training is a bad option. Better to get ahead of it and adjust the strategy in time.

The second lens is the concentration of our income source. How much do we depend on a single source? What happens if it disappears tomorrow?[27] A stable public employee has full concentration but solid architecture. A freelancer anchored to a volatile client has a serious problem, even if the concentration is similar. Moderate concentration is unavoidable for workers who require specific employers, like hospitals or universities, though the work might be transferable to other sectors. For someone building a future, tying themselves to a single income source is outright counterproductive, because fixed conditions don't form the real options that are exactly what they're trying to accumulate.

The third lens is elasticity, which tells us whether we can earn more without selling more hours.[28] If we want free time, the ceiling of fixed hours is a chosen condition. If vocation drives us, elasticity matters only when a lack of resources blocks the task itself, as with the researcher who can't move forward because they depend on an insufficient fixed salary. If we want optionality, an income that grows only by adding hours is a trap. Low elasticity isn't scalable, and every attempt to improve dies against the rigid limit of the day.

---

[27]Christopher B. Barrett, Thomas Reardon, and Patrick Webb, "Nonfarm Income Diversification and Household Livelihood Strategies in Rural Africa: Concepts, Dynamics, and Policy Implications," Food Policy 26, no. 4 (2001): 315–331.
[28]Nassim Nicholas Taleb, The Black Swan: The Impact of the Highly Improbable (New York: Random House, 2007), ch. 3.

Fourth is value updating. Is there a relationship between what the market pays and what we charge?[29] Over the past few decades, productivity and wages, which for a long time grew together, divorced, and much of what work produces stopped showing up in what the worker receives. If we take work as a means, it's enough that it keeps up our purchasing power. Vocation tolerates earning below average, because part of the reward isn't monetary, though there's a point at which earning far below the market average makes even what you love unsustainable. If our priority is the future, a low income can be an acceptable toll, as long as it has an expiration date and doesn't turn into an eternal deferral dressed up as strategy.

The fifth lens reveals our margin of possibility. How many doors could we open that we're not opening today?[30] The right number depends on the lifestyle we want. If we want stability, a thousand geographic or professional options are cognitive noise that breeds anxiety without adding anything, and it always ends up feeling like we're in the wrong place. But professional growth does need the doors to multiply over the years. If after a while the available alternatives aren't growing, the strategy failed.

When these five lenses reveal that the source is misaligned with the life we want, there's no point in going on optimizing expenses or fine-tuning budgets. We have to intervene at the origin, which sometimes means renegotiating terms, sometimes diversifying income, and sometimes simply changing jobs. It isn't always possible right away, of course, but seeing it is the first step toward no longer confusing a problem of life architecture with a spreadsheet problem. If we find a reasonable alignment, we can move on to the next level of visibility, confident we aren't rearranging the chairs while ignoring the elephant in the room.

---

[29] Josh Bivens and Lawrence Mishel, "Understanding the Historic Divergence Between Productivity and a Typical Worker's Pay," Economic Policy Institute Briefing Paper no. 406 (2015).

[30] Nassim Nicholas Taleb, Antifragile: Things That Gain from Disorder (New York: Random House, 2012).

2. The Visibility of Spending

Our grandmothers had no apps, no subaccounts, none of today's colorful charts to put financial life in order, but they had wonderfully effective visibility devices. Think of the jam jar for savings, the cloth envelope for rent, and the notebook full of crooked numbers written in pencil. They watched the money leave and come back, and it was perfectly clear when it was running low and when there was none left. Watching the jar empty out put behavior in order.

Now we have more sophisticated tools, rooted in an invisible economy of automatic payments and installments that dissolve over time. It has its advantages, but it's easier to end up driving at full speed with a fogged-up windshield. We need the clarity of the old systems with the tools of the twenty-first century. So we're going to tune up our visibility devices.

Oddly enough, we have to walk away from the obsessive-tracking approach that promises magic if we leave nothing out. In the end we just exhaust ourselves recording, with no peace, symptoms that lead nowhere. If our fogged-up car is barreling down a mountain road, writing down the numbers on the speedometer is idiotic. First we need to see what's happening outside; only then is the precise speed any help. Let's turn on the defroster.

Here is a critical point worth seeing first. We mostly spend in response to earlier structural decisions that in turn produce cascades of spending. We rent in a certain neighborhood because the price seemed reasonable, but then we spend on transport, on takeout because we get home exhausted, and on health worn down by a sedentary life, because it turns out there's nowhere to walk around there. A plain list records these as isolated expenses, and the gurus keep telling us we're guilty of our bad habits. That is myopia, a failure of visibility. If we look more closely, we see those expenses are born from the decision we made about where to live.

These structural decisions, which also include where we work and on what terms, what domestic infrastructure we have, who we spend time with, and how much energy we have on average, determine total spending before any decision about spending. Daily discipline makes no dent in them, because changing them takes big interventions. In the meantime we can adjust margins, as long as we know what we're dealing with. To see this dimension of spending clearly, we need to ask ourselves three questions periodically.

Which structural decisions generate the biggest spending cascades for us? We look at the five most significant recurring expenses and trace each one back to the original decision that makes it unavoidable. Outsourced laundry, for example, comes from not having invested in a washing machine, and the spending on expensive outings comes from our social circle. Going from symptom to cause, we don't waste time trying to change behaviors that run deeper than habit.

Do we want to keep those decisions? If the answer is yes, let's accept the cost without guilt and without complaint. Maybe living far away keeps us close to family, and that's a conscious, coherent decision. If we want to change them, the intervention has to aim at the structural decision, and only then will the cascade disappear.

If we do want to change, in the meantime, which aspect of that change is most feasible? By identifying which aspect would cut the most spending with the least effort, we can concentrate energy instead of scattering ourselves trying to discipline many expenses at once.

Only at this point, when we know where we stand, do we reach the place where tracking makes sense.

When we look beneath the structural decisions at the daily flow of purchases, outings, and consumption that fill out the month, we find they don't all serve the same function, which is why blending them into a single mass makes everything opaque. We're back to copying the numbers off the speedometer. When we instead let the expenses show themselves without crushing them into one category, they appear organized into three zones:

The control zone includes everything that holds up the concrete structure of our current life: housing, utilities, basic food, transport, and obligations that can't be put off. It's the floor that keeps everything standing.

The living zone holds what we need beyond subsistence to make the present livable. Enjoyment, rest, and some overspending go in here.

The future zone covers what doesn't exist yet but we're building: savings, investments, the projects we're betting on, and the safety cushion.

This basic distinction lets us quickly see what function each expense is serving and, above all, as we'll see, where the system is getting out of order. This multiplicity calls for organizing information on movements and trends so we don't depend on discipline or memory. To be useful, it can't be a mere record; it has to be a visibility map that shows how well the allocation method we've chosen is working. But how do you choose?

3. Budget: The Operating System of Financial Life

The visibility map we just mentioned is what we usually call a budget. The name sounds stern, but it's a tool designed to make decisions our future self will thank us for.

Budgets are usually expressed in percentages, for good reasons that grew out of a historical answer to a concrete problem. Money changes magnitude all the time, while life keeps its proportions. Thinking about a budget in percentages captures that relative constancy without getting trapped in rigid numbers that age badly. The idea was born in household accounting and public administration.

In the early twentieth century, when industrial wages began to stabilize and urban families had relatively steady cash income, the first studies of family economics in the United States and Europe noticed that families organized their spending in implicit proportions.[31] Instead of saying "I spend this much," they preferred to put it as something being "too much for us" or "going over our margin." Over time, that intuition got formalized into proportional schemes that let people adjust without redoing everything each month.

Later, macroeconomics and corporate planning reinforced this logic. Corporate budgets and even tax systems work the same way, because it's a way of seeing the structure. When we bring this logic to personal life, we treat it with the seriousness decisions deserve.

When people talk about models like 50/30/20 or 60/20/20, each figure reflects the three kinds of spending we've seen: control, life, and future. Each one organizes money in a particular way, prioritizing a specific tension according to our goals and our income. Some keep the balance, others protect against volatility, and some are designed to accelerate change or head off collapse. There's no single correct model in the abstract, since at different stages of life we may need different ones.

Suppose we're in a stable moment. The 50/30/20 model can work well if our income and expenses are steady. It was popularized in the 2000s by the senator and scholar Elizabeth Warren, long before she was known for politics, as a way to translate into everyday rules something household economics already knew.[32] It assigns roughly half to basic needs, 30 percent explicitly to lifestyle, and locks in 20 percent for saving. It tends to be sustainable, a model built to last and to keep pace with real life

---

[31] Ernst Engel, "Die Produktions- und Consumtionsverhältnisse des Königreichs Sachsen," Zeitschrift des Statistischen Bureaus des Königlich Sächsischen Ministeriums des Innern 3 (1857): 1–54; and Frédéric Le Play, Les ouvriers européens: Études sur les travaux, la vie domestique et la condition morale des populations ouvrières de l'Europe (Paris: Imprimerie Impériale, 1855).

[32] Elizabeth Warren and Amelia Warren Tyagi, All Your Worth: The Ultimate Lifetime Money Plan (New York: Free Press, 2005).

without generating constant friction. Its limit shows up when you're after a quick jump or a structural transformation. In those cases, the balance that makes it livable also makes it slow.

Now think of a situation with variable income. Here the 60/20/20 scheme usually adapts better, which is why so many freelancers prefer it. It forces you not to spend in the good months as if they were permanent, holding the surplus for leaner times. At first glance it looks more wasteful because it allots more to needs, but it's a defensive strategy. With variable income, many things that would be "lifestyle" under a stable scheme come to be experienced as necessities, like higher rent so you don't have to move often, redundant services, work tools, and operating cushions. We buy stability, because when life is irregular, keeping up the basics costs more.

What if we're committed to a big change? The 40/30/30 model, which goes beyond balance to accelerate accumulation, since it devotes an unusually high share to saving and investing as a strategic bet. Historically it's also used in high-volatility economies, where waiting for "better conditions" tends to be an elegant way of never moving forward. It demands more discipline and a higher tolerance for a tight short term, but it turns transformation into a tangible budget priority. It's hard as a way of life, but ideal for a stage of growth.

It can also happen that we're in open emergency. In those cases we can reach for the 70/20/10 scheme. It spread in the '80s and '90s, when consumer credit went mass-market and brought cycles of household over-indebtedness with it. It's a plan for moments of crisis, with debt out of control, lost income, separations, illness, or forced moves. It works like a financial cast that limits movement. It's uncomfortable and ugly, but it holds everything in place until recovery arrives. When it stretches beyond a short term, though, it stops being therapeutic and becomes anesthesia.

Described this way, these budget models look like technical tools we choose rationally. But behind each model sits our financial signature, which tends toward the scheme that confirms its dominant bias rather than the one that best protects us. So when choosing a model, we have to weigh our goals and the stage of life, while watching which one our signature is pushing us toward, to make sure it isn't the signature running the choice.

The Accumulator, governed by loss aversion and not quite telling real danger from groundless fear, tends to live in permanent emergency. Even with no objective crisis, their daily setup looks like a silent 70/20/10 where the "needs" grow until they absorb any margin and saving acts as a defensive wall. The sense of control is reassuring, but at the cost of a narrow life. They should move to a livable scheme (50/30/20 or 60/20/20) that keeps the saving while switching off the vigilance and lets them spend without feeling they're betraying something essential.

At the opposite extreme is the Compensator, hit by present bias. On paper they tend to sign up for balanced budgets, even demanding ones, but in practice the scheme falls apart when tiredness or the need for reward shows up. At that point the lifestyle share expands and the rest withers. The solution is automation mechanisms, as we saw in ARCO, not a restrictive budget. A well-implemented 60/20/20 can fit them better than any promise of self-control, turning the impulse into a contained variable.

The Avoider doesn't lean toward any model, because they don't want to hear about budgets. Present bias works passively as chronic delay, so they live with a residual budget made of urgent payments and deferred decisions. For this profile, any complex scheme is doomed to be abandoned. What can work, instead, is a simple, almost invisible model, with few categories and strong automation. A 60/20/20 with minimal review, or even a 50/30/20 stripped of friction, can give back predictability without distress.

The Controller is usually drawn to demanding models, like the 40/30/30, by the illusion that if everything is well assigned and watched, nothing bad will happen. Loss aversion combines with the illusion of control, and they experience every deviation as a personal failure. The adjustment lies in trusting the system more than constant supervision. It helps to remember that a somewhat less aggressive but more sustainable scheme tends to produce better long-term results than a flawless architecture that wears them out.

The Optimist, ruled by the private conviction that the future will be more orderly and will absorb the present's excesses, tends to pick aspirational budgets, assuming income that doesn't exist yet or projecting peaks that aren't permanent. Schemes that introduce an automatic brake, like the 60/20/20, are especially useful here, because they turn optimism into reserves without snuffing out the creative drive that defines them.

The Protector, finally, tends to live in emergency budgets without recognizing them as such. The funds for lifestyle or saving get absorbed by help and emotional commitments presented as unavoidable. The sunk-cost fallacy leads them to keep putting in resources because they've already put so much into building their generous image. The budget is organized around others, which is why it's fragile, whatever the model. Explicit boundaries, so that caretaking doesn't colonize the whole architecture, are the priority.

With clear visibility over income and spending, and a budget model suited to our situation and aligned with our financial signature, we can now build the budget: intelligence applied to our own life.

4. Building the Budget

Budgets come in many shapes, but they all share the same four movements: look, decide, implement, correct. Each one needs the one before it to work, and skipping one is the most common cause of failure.

First movement: diagnosis. We need to know how much it costs to be us. That real version shows up when we look at three months of bank statements or expense records without editing the story.

This diagnosis has two layers. The first is the structure. It includes housing, utilities, basic food, health, transport, education, all the obligations that don't depend on our mood or our level of motivation. Those expenses keep existing even if we stay in bed a whole week. Some people think they spend little because they don't notice the installments debiting on their own, the insurance no one reviews, and the subscriptions that outlived the curiosity that created them. Others think they spend a lot because they lump everything together without distinguishing what they choose from what simply happens. The monthly average, not the best month and not the worst, is the number that tells the truth. Platforms like YNAB or Monarch Money let you import transactions and categorize them automatically. Even a Google Sheets connected to bank data can do it with reasonable precision. A well-used AI can surface forgotten subscriptions, duplicate payments, and seasonal patterns the human eye takes months to catch. The tool is secondary as long as we arrive at a clear number.

The second layer is more delicate, because it asks us to look at the life we choose when we have room. Here come the outings, the treats, the cultural consumption, the trips, and above all those expenses that appear when we're tense or looking for relief. This layer calls for honesty in telling what gives us lasting wellbeing from what works as momentary anesthesia. Would we choose this expense again if it were less frequent? If the answer is yes, it's part of the chosen life and deserves its place in the budget without guilt. If the answer is "it depends how my week went," it's an emotional expense that needs to be recognized as such, because the way to manage it is different. Now, let's remember that each signature distorts what it sees. If they look closely, the Compensator will find more emotional than functional expenses in this layer; the Accumulator will discover that their "chosen life" is suspiciously austere out of pure fear, and the same goes for the rest. Knowing this before we look is an advantage: the lucidity to tell diagnosis from self-deception.

From the subtraction between what comes in and what both layers cost, the real margin emerges. It isn't "what's left over," an expression that already carries the resignation that nothing will be left. The real margin is our room to maneuver: to save, absorb the unexpected, and build a future. Many people live for years without knowing this number and yet make complex financial decisions blind, like driving at night with no headlights and trusting the road will be straight. Sometimes it is. Often it isn't. It can also happen that the diagnosis reveals there's no margin. That's a hard moment, but it's better to know it sooner rather than later, instead of going on financing the fiction with debt or with sheer hope. That knowledge lets us intervene on the architecture or revisit the chosen life. Either way, the diagnosis did its job of making visible what was operating in the dark.

Second movement: design. With the margin on the table and the goals we already defined in N, now we have to decide which distribution model will sustain them. Conventional methods separate the steps (goals first, then the model) as if they were independent, but that's a mistake. Back to Ana. Her real margin, after the diagnosis, is $800 a month. Her priority goal is the $12,000 emergency fund in 24 months, which needs between $400 and $600 a month according to the range Realism calibrated. That leaves her between $200 and $400 for the other two goals and for any surprise that doesn't count as an emergency. With that margin, a 40/30/30 is mathematically possible but psychologically unworkable, because it would force her to compress her chosen life to a point that, being a Compensator, will blow up in the first hard month. A 50/30/20, by contrast, gives her room to live without guilt and channel almost the entire 20 percent of future into the fund, with a minimal remainder for a second medium-term goal. The mechanism matters, because Ana needs the saving to come out first and automatically. If it's left for "after spending," her signature will do what it always does. The model and the goal need each other. Decide them together or the whole thing falls apart.

The simplest model is usually the one that works best, because complexity sabotages follow-through. Each extra category is an extra decision, and we already know what happens to decisions when they pile up. If after three months we find we need more detail in some area, only then do we add that category.

One more thing is worth spelling out: every use of money forecloses another. What we spend on one thing disappears and can't be used on another. Making the trade-off that grounds the design explicit, by writing it down, for example, next to a goal for the year as an acknowledgment of limits, reduces frustration and removes the vague sense of "failing" when we're actually choosing. "I can't afford to travel" is different from "this year I chose to prioritize the emergency fund and put off the trip."

Third movement: implementation. The designed budget has to come down to earth, and for that it takes the form of a dashboard. That dashboard, the place where all the information converges so we can read it effortlessly, doesn't need to be sophisticated, but it does have to be consistent. There's no need to set up anything new, because it's the same tools we already used in the diagnosis, the ones that import and categorize transactions automatically. What changes is the function, and that change reorders something we said earlier. In the diagnosis we held that the tool was secondary as long as we reached a clear number, and that was true, because we were taking a one-time snapshot and it didn't matter which camera. In implementation the tool matters, because it's no longer a snapshot but a habit sustained over time, and whether we keep using it depends on how comfortable it is. A comfortable tool feeds itself; an uncomfortable one gets dropped by the second month, and an abandoned dashboard gives no visibility. The ideal is automatic sync from the bank or from an app that aggregates accounts, with categorization we only review when it fails, because the less manual effort it demands, the more likely the habit survives. Recording each expense by hand isn't impossible, but it's what most people abandon, so choose the tool you'll still be using six months from now, not the most powerful one.

What does the dashboard record? It can't be a mere list of transactions, however tidy. To work, it has to have assigned categories and limits for each, starting from four basic elements: the name of the expense and its zone (control, life, or future), the assigned budget, what's been spent so far, and the remaining balance.

On that base we can add two layers that enrich the map without complicating it. The first marks progress (how much of that category's budget has been used), something automated apps handle with colored bars. The second, more valuable and less common, is a brief note on the emotional origin of an expense, where it applies. This layer improves the quality of the record for transactions we recognize as tied to stress or boredom. It doesn't change the number, but it changes what we understand of it. No more is needed. In fact, the more loaded the dashboard, the less we use it.

Every bit of automation helps. That automation is the concrete expression of everything we designed in ARCO's systemic Orchestration: the functional separation of accounts, payment calendars, and budget hierarchies. It's best to automate first what's hardest to do by hand, because that's where friction reveals its real weight. If every month we struggle to decide how much to transfer to savings, that decision is badly made, and if every month we recalculate how much is left to spend, the system isn't doing its job. In short, the implementation is good if, once everything is set up, the only thing that needs conscious attention is discretionary spending, because everything else we already decided before we needed to decide it.

Fourth movement: review. A budget that goes unwatched quietly becomes fiction. The gap accumulates in silence until one day the budget and the life are two stories that don't recognize each other. Review exists to prevent that divorce, but it has to calibrate its own intensity well. Too much control turns the budget into an unbearable boss and we end up dropping it from exhaustion. With too little contact, the system goes out of date without our noticing, as happens to the Avoider. The right frequency depends on the profile, but two rituals work as a minimum structure for any signature.

The first is weekly and lasts five minutes. Its only aim is to take the pulse: how much is left in the operating account? Is the main limit still holding? Just observe: no judgment, no interpretation. This is not the moment to fix anything.

The second is monthly and lasts about fifteen minutes. First we look at whether the proportion between control, life, and future matches the budget. We notice if Control is eating more than planned, if Life is overflowing through some emotional pattern the budget didn't account for, or if Future shrank or vanished. An isolated deviation says nothing. Three months telling the same story justify revising the budget. Then we focus on the fine grain, watching the Life expenses and the Control commitments that might have slipped in by inertia. Two questions are enough. Is this a habit or an accident? If something shows up week after week, even in small amounts, it's already a pattern the budget needs to absorb or neutralize. Does this answer a need or an emotion? An expense with a concrete function isn't handled the same way as one that anesthetizes us. If it's recurring, as we saw in the counter-sabotages of N, the environment has to be redesigned so it doesn't require willpower.

A good way to close each monthly review is to ask ourselves what we learned about how we decide. The focus shifts off the numbers, guilt drops away, and in its place we gain knowledge about how we function under pressure. Over time, these answers become the kind of practical wisdom no app can offer.

* * *

Visibility is what lets us stop guessing and start deciding. Once the diagnosis is done, the budget designed, and the dashboard running, we ask what to do with what we see. The margin we identified, that muscle we've started to exercise, still has no instructions. How much of that margin turns into savings? If there are debts, do we pay them first or save in parallel? When does it make sense to make the leap from saving to investing? And how do we do all this without confusing strategy with a gamble? These questions aren't answered by looking at the dashboard but by thinking like strategists. That's what we'll take up in E.

E

Engineering

In 1978, Reinhold Messner climbed Everest without supplemental oxygen. The mountaineering community said it was impossible. Everyone knew that above 8,000 meters the human body can't cope without help. Messner, though, designed a strategy that didn't depend on what was missing. He cut weight to the minimum, stripped away everything nonessential, picked a precise weather window, and organized an acclimatization the other expeditions found excessive. While the others climbed fast, loaded with gear and oxygen, Messner climbed slow and prepared.

The market is our mountain. With no will of its own and nothing against us, it stands in front of us, enormous and full of conditions we don't control. If we have resources to spare for the heavy-gear ascent, we can eye Messner sideways; if we don't, we aren't condemned to be spectators either. We can design our expedition with the resources we have, adapting to conditions rather than giving up and preparing for the difficult moments that inevitable come.

What we've already built corresponds to the first two phases of any serious expedition. In N we designed the route and the climbing plan, with the camps we want to reach, fully aware of the capacities we have. We know how much altitude we tolerate and where we tend to make mistakes; we have logistics, contingency plans for bad weather, and plans for the dangerous stretches. In V we fine-tuned the survey of the terrain and the supply lines. The diagnosis of income and spending is our map of slopes and distances. No serious climber goes up without one, but we're still at base camp. What comes now, in E, is the climb itself.

Our strategy rests on three elements. Saving gives us the secure points where we can take shelter when the weather worsens. Without base camps there's no expedition. No one wants to carry debt, but it's sometimes an indispensable part of the gear we haul. Think of Messner: the gear has to help us climb, not weight us down. Finally, investment pushes us toward the summit. It always involves risk to reach what looked like a distant silhouette, but it's our toll to the goal. Each element needs different conditions and tolerances, which is why we have to know them well before thinking about the sophisticated tools we'll load into the pack. Messner didn't climb Everest with the same gear we take on a weekend trek, but he didn't carry anything superfluous either. In the same way, accounts, funds, bonds, and instruments are tools for specific conditions, chosen for what each one adds once we know how our strategy works, not because fashion dictates it. So let's organize the hard part of our expedition.

1. From Saver to Strategist

"Saving is the foundation of wealth" once sounded like an almost self-evident principle. In part it was. It worked fairly well in societies with relatively stable wages and predictable working lives. Saving meant deferring present consumption to build future security in an environment where the future kept a certain continuity with the present. The problem is that much of that has disappeared.

The first difficulty is that saving stopped depending on individual will alone. For decades you could sustain the idea that discipline and effort were enough to build economic stability. Today that relationship is far more uncertain. The costs of housing, health, and education grew in many places faster than wages, while work became more precarious and intermittent. Many people live too close to their limits. Under those conditions, turning saving into a purely moral matter, as if everything depended on "getting your act together," is simplistic and sometimes cruel. The ability to save is deeply conditioned by economic structures outside our control.

The second difficulty is deeper still. Contemporary wealth often comes less from saving than from owning assets. Over recent decades, a large part of the growth in net worth came from the appreciation of homes, stocks, and other financial instruments. Two equally disciplined people can end up in completely different situations depending on whether they got access to certain assets at the right moment. Someone who bought a home before a big real-estate run-up, for instance, can multiply their net worth without having saved any more than others over the years. So saving is still important, but it no longer explains wealth accumulation on its own. It always operates inside a wider system of unequal access to opportunity and assets.

For its part, the old gospel of saving assumed a relatively predictable world of work. The classic financial recommendations, from how much to set aside for emergencies to what share of income to reserve, start from stable careers and relatively calculable risks. In a context marked by recurring crises, accelerated technological change, shifts in the labor market, and rising uncertainty, they tell us little, on top of the fact that there are no universal formulas valid for everyone. For some people, an emergency fund of a few months can be enough; for others, even several years of savings could evaporate fast in the face of an illness, a forced move, or a prolonged loss of income. The real problem is that the very horizon of predictability has become more fragile.

None of this touches the relevance of saving. It remains a central tool of autonomy and protection against uncertainty. We just have to drop the simplistic narrative that puts it all on discipline, because contemporary economic reality is quite a bit more complex.

It seems silly to clarify what saving is, but we carry around some fairly mistaken ideas. The image of the piggy bank triggers the split between money spent and money saved, as if any sum that doesn't leave the account immediately automatically joined the second category. Between the two there's a much more ambiguous zone. A good part of the money we think is "saved" is in fact already committed. When we set money aside for taxes, insurance, tuition, a booked vacation, or foreseeable expenses in the coming months, that money already has a destination. Money in transit like that isn't available to reorganize our life or to absorb uncertainty. It looks still, but it's really just waiting for the moment to leave. Real saving begins only when money takes on the job of sustaining stability and cushioning blows, widening our room to act in the future.

Many people overestimate their stability because they see a positive balance and feel relief, when in fact they don't have that money. When an illness, a major repair, a drop in income, or simply a stretch of exhaustion that forces them to slow down breaks the calendar, the "saved" money disappears in a few days, because it had never truly left the circuit of current spending. Real saving is the building of margin, never simply the accumulation of a balance.

Most serious financial problems show up when we live too close to our own limits. When we have no margin, a late payment or an unexpected expense produces disproportionate effects, because the whole personal system runs at the edge of saturation. Under those conditions money becomes a permanent source of tension. That's why the first aim of saving is to reduce fragility. Before thinking about net worth or growth, we need to build some distance from constant emergency, the real beginning of autonomy.

The budget we built in V already decided which part of income belongs to the future. The strategic question now is how to organize that flow. The most common mistake is to treat all saving as if it served the same function, because different kinds of saving manage different risks, which is why it's worth organizing them in layers.

The first layer is the emergency fund. Its function is to protect the continuity of the system, keeping a relatively short interruption from destroying the whole balance of our personal finances. The emergency fund prioritizes availability and immediate liquidity over growth. This matters especially in inflationary or monetarily unstable contexts. Many people judge the cushion with an investment logic and end up putting it in instruments that are too volatile or hard to liquidate. An emergency fund isn't there to maximize net worth. It buys time and protects the system's other layers. Without it, any surprise forces us to destroy other reserves, liquidating investments at the wrong moment or going into debt. The cushion is unproductive, and that's exactly as it should be.

When someone has no cushion, they live in a logic of immediate crisis resolution. Under those conditions it's very hard to make rational long-term decisions, because almost all mental energy is absorbed by urgency. When we start from zero, the priority should be to gather even one month of basic expenses through the automation we built in N. It sounds like little, but even a minimal cushion produces an important shift. One month of margin changes the relationship with money, because it changes the daily perception of risk. Little by little, the possibility appears of waiting, negotiating, or even saying no, and that changes decisions at a deeper level.

When that first layer reaches some stability, room begins to open for goal-based saving. Here money is aimed at producing concrete and relatively predictable changes. A fund for a home, a move, professional training, work equipment, or a personal project works very differently from an abstract account simply called "savings." Specific goals sustain the effort better, because they connect the present to a visible transformation.

This matters because saving isn't only rational calculation. It also means handling anxiety, and it depends on our perception of time. We fail at saving not from ignorance of basic math but because the future feels too abstract or uncertain to justify sustained sacrifices in the present. When the horizon is completely blurred, we feel saving as permanent deprivation with no perceptible reward.[33] That's why intermediate goals tend to work better than the excessively distant ones. A horizon of two to five years keeps enough distance to demand consistency, but enough emotional closeness to hold psychological meaning. Saving needs a certain connection with our future self, and when that connection disappears, even disciplined people throw in the towel.

Only after the first two layers reach some stability does saving for investment appear. Here the logic changes again. This third layer seeks to widen future possibilities. Money begins to operate offensively, acquiring assets and expanding net worth over time. Now, precisely because this layer promises visible growth, it tends to produce serious mistakes. Contemporary financial culture makes investment glamorous and the cushion boring. The result is that many people try to build wealth on extremely fragile structures. As long as the context cooperates, all goes well, but if a real shock arrives, unemployment, illness, sharp inflation, or a market drop, you have to turn long-term assets into immediate liquidity to cover basic expenses. What looked like solid growth reveals itself as a structure with no shock absorber.

In short, a financial strategy's quality is measured first by how much it can withstand imperfect scenarios without falling apart, and only then by how much it can grow. Financial success consists,

---

[33]Hal Hershfield, Your Future Self: How to Make Tomorrow Better Today (New York: Little, Brown Spark, 2023). See also Hal E. Hershfield et al., "Increasing Saving Behavior Through Age-Progressed Renderings of the Future Self," Journal of Marketing Research 48, no. SPL (2011): S23–S37.

quietly, in building a system able to sustain continuity without forcing us to start from zero again and again.

2. Debt and the Colonization of the Future

Debt is, in essence, a time machine, and like every time machine it produces strange paradoxes. When we take on debt, we tear a portion of money out of the future and drag it into the present. We live today on resources we haven't generated yet, as if a future version of ourselves had sent resources back to us without quite explaining the cost of returning them. The initial feeling is usually expansive. All at once an advance version of our future life materializes in the now. But the movement through time doesn't stop there. When we begin to repay the debt, the direction reverses. The present starts working to pay for decisions fixed in the past. Each installment is a fragment of present time sacrificed to sustain a choice that can no longer be changed. There appears one of debt's most unsettling oddities: the past keeps material power over us long after it has vanished.

This is why long debts produce such a particular psychological feeling. More than money owed, they are futures partly occupied in advance. Months or years that haven't arrived yet already have an owner. Part of our salary three years from now may already be committed today to pay for something that might even have stopped mattering to us.

When we look at the outstanding balance, something stranger still happens. In a single figure, three time frames overlap. Past, present, and future overlap in a single figure: the original decision condensed, the concrete weight of installments felt now, and the shadow of payments that don't yet exist but already limit what's possible. The temporal structure of regret shows up transformed into a bank statement.

Debt, however, isn't necessarily a mistake. Some of the most important transformations of a life would be impossible without it. A home, the expansion of a project, or even survival in hard contexts often require bringing future resources into the present. The problem is losing sight of its temporal nature as a contract between different versions of ourselves. As in almost every time-travel story, the danger appears when the future ends up paying far more than the past imagined.

This temporal and emotional density makes simplistic approaches to debt especially inadequate. The moralist presents it as an ethical fall that must be purged through sacrifice, turning each installment into penance. In German, Schuld means both debt and guilt, a sign that owing money and owing morally are experiences the brain never fully separated. Many languages do something similar. From the Code of Hammurabi and Deuteronomy we find ritual limits on the accumulation of debt and cycles of forgiveness, because the problem was never only economic. Debt touches something ancestral, that sense that someone now holds rights over time we haven't yet lived and that we ourselves pledged.

The technocrat, for their part, reduces it to a variable to optimize by calculating rates, as if the problem were purely arithmetic. The superficial behaviorist reads it as a lack of self-control or a craving for immediate gratification, ignoring that often going into debt is simply the best available option, or even the only one. All three perspectives capture real fragments of the phenomenon, but none describes it whole, for what it is: a technology for managing intertemporal uncertainty that works as long as we don't lose control and start mortgaging ever more distant futures to prop up ever more fragile presents.

The interest rate occupies a central place in this dynamic because it represents, at bottom, the price of time. The lender hands over resources today in exchange for recovering more tomorrow. That price is never neutral. It depends on risk, on inflation, on bargaining power, and often on the borrower's degree of desperation. The more vulnerable someone is, the more dearly they tend to pay for access to the future. With assets, stability, and a spotless credit history, we can get cheap time, while someone living on the edge of urgency will pay through the nose. Credit cards, fast-cash loans, and payday loans are destructive when they sell time under extreme conditions. The more suffocated a person is, the less able they are to negotiate the price of that time.

In situations of exhaustion or late payments, the problem starts to feel like an urgent need for air. A "tiny" installment or an instant approval that lets you put the matter off a few days produces instant emotional relief, and the brain stops weighing how much that purchased time will really cost. These instruments work so well because they fragment the financial pain into small, repeated, relatively invisible withdrawals. The person doesn't feel one big blow but a slow erosion of interest charges that show up every month, automatic refinancings, minimum payments that look manageable, and balances that never quite disappear. The problem is that the purchased time starts multiplying future debt much faster than it generates real capacity to repay it, and then debt stops being a temporal bridge and progressively colonizes the future.

Inflation adds another temporal oddity. In inflationary contexts, debts change meaning over time. A fixed-rate debt can be diluted until it becomes relatively light if income keeps pace with inflation. An indexed or variable debt, by contrast, can turn into an explosive trap. This means the temporal experience of debt also depends on the monetary regime where it exists. A thirty-year mortgage doesn't mean the same thing in Switzerland, Argentina, or Turkey. The same installments can represent reasonable stability or a permanent threat of collapse that has us living on a roller coaster.

Different debts manage different risks and occupy the future in different ways. Debt aimed at investing in future capacity, for example, seeks to increase our generation of income. It can finance human capital (education, specialized training, professional instruction) or productive capital: machinery, tools, inventory, infrastructure. In both cases the aim is for the future to produce more resources than are needed to repay the debt, but even here the risks differ. Human capital becomes part of ourselves and no one can fully seize it, though its returns tend to be uncertain and slow. A huge educational debt for a profession with no economic prospects can turn into toxic debt even if the learning was valuable on other planes. Productive debt, by contrast, can generate quick returns, but it depends on the survival of the business it finances.

Asset debt occupies another zone. It finances tangible assets that remain after payment and reorganize daily stability. Homeownership is the paradigmatic case. A mortgage commits cash flow for decades in exchange for housing stability and some protection from the volatility of rents. It works especially well when the architecture of life requires prolonged geographic permanence and there's enough income stability to sustain long installments without constant suffocation. Some goods stay in gray zones. A car can be productive capital if it lets you work or reach opportunities otherwise impossible, but it can also function simply as emotionally rationalized consumer debt. The difference matters, because we often present as "investment" what is really financed desire.

Consumer debt, precisely, is probably the most demonized category and yet one of the most unavoidable. A large part of contemporary life runs on consumption brought forward through installments, cards, and everyday financing. Few people could furnish a house, get through a move, replace a broken appliance, or even sustain certain standards of living by paying for everything in cash. In many cases going into debt is simply the least bad way to get through temporary liquidity constraints or to spread large expenses over time without destroying the monthly flow. Still, when credit finances basic expenses month after month, we're no longer bringing forward exceptional consumption but using the future to prop up a present that can't sustain itself.

Emotional debt is especially dangerous. We already saw in I that there are relatively stable financial signatures. When those dynamics combine with credit, the result can turn explosive. The

Compensator, for instance, uses debt to produce immediate relief from frustration or exhaustion. The Avoider goes into debt when they can no longer keep putting off hard decisions. The Optimist brings forward imaginary futures out of enthusiasm and underestimates real risks. The Protector can quietly mortgage themselves to support others while their own stability deteriorates. In all these cases debt rarely springs from cold financial calculation. Instead, it appears tied to intense emotional states that later get retrospective rational justifications. We all know people who understand rates, installments, and interest perfectly and still repeat destructive patterns because of the psychological function debt serves.

Finally there's toxic debt, the kind that stops financing the present or the future and starts simply sustaining earlier debt. We refinance minimum payments endlessly while the balance grows from compound interest, or we use credit to cover basic expenses recurrently without changing the system's overall architecture. At that point debt hides the structural collapse.

Debts take shape in concrete instruments, from a mortgage to a credit card, that commit the future in different ways.

The credit card is the most widespread debt instrument in formalized economies. Its design is brilliant from the issuer's point of view and dangerous for the user, because it fragments the temporal cost until it becomes almost invisible.[34] The purchase happens today, but the financial impact shows up distributed across small future payments that rarely feel connected to the original decision. This works so well because the human brain perceives one big single payment far more intensely than ten small ones spread over time, even if the total cost is identical or greater. Installments reduce the "pain of paying" because they separate consumption from its corresponding economic sacrifice. The problem is that the future starts to fill silently with simultaneous

---

[34]Neil Stewart, "The Cost of Anchoring on Credit-Card Minimum Repayments," Psychological Science 20, no. 1 (2009): 39–41.

micro-commitments. Each purchase looks reasonable on its own: a phone, a repair, clothes, a flight, every decision isolated while the debt piles up, and suddenly we discover we've turned a good part of next year's income into money in transit…

The idea, constantly repeated in the media and in moralizing talk, that using a card or paying in installments is automatically a sign of financial crisis is fairly simplistic. Many people with stable income and enough liquidity use credit simply to organize their spending over time or to keep margin available. In high-inflation economies, it can even be rational to pay in installments while having the money on hand, because the real value of those installments tends to erode over time. The situation changes completely when we stop paying the full balance and start refinancing. There the card turns into revolving debt. The minimum payment, one of the great psychological inventions of contemporary finance, turns a visible crisis into a slow, seemingly manageable erosion until compound interest destroys everything.

Personal loans produce a different temporal experience, since they make visible from the start how much future time we're committing. We know how much we'll pay, for how long, and the terms are clear. That clarity has something brutal but also something healthy. The total financial cost matters far more than the advertised rate. It's worth remembering that the visible interest often looks reasonable, but mandatory insurance, administrative fees, and commissions turn the loan into something much more expensive than it seemed.

At the most aggressive end come fast-cash loans and payday loans. These instruments sell time under extreme conditions. The more suffocated a person is, the less able they are to negotiate the price of that time. There appears one of the cruelest asymmetries of the financial system: those who most need immediate relief tend to get the money on the worst possible terms. Urgency always destroys the capacity to negotiate over time.

Debts rarely start out toxic. The most common thing is for them to degrade slowly. A manageable installment or an occasional refinancing don't, on their own, destroy a financial architecture. If this becomes the norm, the purchased time no longer generates future expansion or stability, and our mental energy gets absorbed by constant calculations, postponements, anticipatory anxiety, and a sense of being chased through time. Many very intelligent people make disastrous financial decisions when they enter debt spirals. In these cases, surface solutions usually fail. When a financial architecture collapses, “organizing better” or cutting small symbolic expenses isn't enough. Often the problem requires structural changes, raising income, sharply reducing fixed commitments, selling assets, renegotiating, or even legally restructuring debt. The sooner the snowball is stopped, the better.

Every debt depends far less on its absolute size than on the architecture that has to sustain it. The same installment can be almost imperceptible for one person and completely suffocating for another. Some people live calmly owing enormous sums and others go into crisis with relatively modest commitments, because what matters is the margin left after paying the debts. This shows up in two concepts. On one hand, debt capacity indicates how much temporal commitment our income and spending structure can reasonably sustain before it starts becoming fragile. On the other, debt load shows how much of that capacity is already taken. What matters here is the distance between the two. As long as there's room between load and capacity, the system keeps its elasticity, but if that distance shrinks too far, we run out of margin and any weak month or unexpected expense feels like a bomb.

For this reason the stability of income matters as much as the amount earned. With a stable salary, a high installment can be perfectly sustainable, while a much smaller one can become a permanent source of tension for a freelancer with variable income. The whole difference lies in the uncertainty our financial architecture can absorb without breaking. The financial system institutionalizes this logic through credit-scoring mechanisms. FICO scores, credit reports, or any equivalent work, at bottom, as systems that assess how reliable we are at managing the future. The system rewards those who sustain temporal commitments consistently and penalizes those who show discontinuity or fragility. Our access to credit and the price of time depend increasingly on that quantified temporal reputation. This produces the paradox that to get better debt terms we first have to demonstrate the ability to handle debt. That's why a card used responsibly can be useful even for someone who doesn't need immediate financing, because the system reads a consistent history as a sign of temporal stability.

Many initially reasonable debts become destructive because the context that sustained them changed. A perfectly manageable mortgage between two people can turn suffocating after a divorce. A loan taken with stable income can become dangerous after unemployment, illness, or a sharp drop in economic activity. This matters because we tend to judge financial decisions in hindsight as if the future context had been foreseeable, when much financial fragility appears precisely because life changes faster than long debt structures. Intervening early matters. The sooner we recognize that the original architecture no longer exists, the more options remain available. Selling an asset, renegotiating terms, extending timelines, or reducing commitments is usually far less destructive than waiting until the edge of collapse, trying to prop up a structure that no longer matches our reality.

Something similar happens with cosigners. To cosign is to take on potential debt without controlling the use of the money or the behavior of the main borrower. The bank lends time using our future as backing. Since the risk stays invisible while everything works, many people enormously underestimate the responsibility they take on by signing.

There's a point where the logic of holding on stops making sense. If the total debt clearly exceeds our capacity to pay and informal renegotiation fails, artificially sustaining the system can make things much worse. Banks usually have more room to negotiate than they admit at first, because they often prefer to renegotiate rather than go through long, costly court processes.

But renegotiating doesn't simply mean lowering installments. A refinancing that reduces the monthly payment by hugely extending the timeline can worsen the total cost and prolong a state of fragility for years. A truly useful renegotiation improves the overall architecture: it lowers rates, freezes interest, restructures principal, or returns operating margin.

When even that fails, insolvency appears. Bankruptcy or insolvency proceedings, depending on the jurisdiction, exist because legal systems recognize that there are situations where a debt stops being payable without completely destroying the debtor's economic life. Insolvency shouldn't be romanticized or used as a trivial escape mechanism, but neither should it be understood as absolute moral failure. Sometimes it's simply the formal recognition that the committed future far exceeds the real capacity to sustain it.

There's also an inverse form of financial distortion, the compulsive need to eliminate all debt as fast as possible even if that destroys our liquidity or our quality of life. Some people can't psychologically tolerate owing money even when it would financially make sense to live with certain relatively cheap debts while building savings or investment. Debt does produce worry, and many people feel enormous emotional relief when they recover a sense of available future, so wanting to end it is understandable, unless it leads to economically irrational decisions. A mortgage at a rate below inflation, for example, can shrink on its own in real terms while the available capital produces much more value invested elsewhere. It's worth insisting that the much-repeated linear sequence of eliminating all debt, then saving, and finally investing doesn't always work. It depends on many factors: real rates, inflation, income stability, age, psychological tolerance, and available opportunities. Often the soundest strategy is to build a cushion, reduce expensive debt, and invest gradually, all at the same time.

Every debt is, in the end, a negotiation between different versions of ourselves. Some expand our future possibilities.

Others slowly occupy them until they become uninhabitable. If we're going to step into the time machine, it's worth being sure how much future we're willing to put at stake.

3. The INVERSO Engine

Suppose now that we have enough savings and no expensive debt. Inflation rises, faster or slower, and keeping money still means losing it in slow motion. That available money can move without throwing us into disorder, moving from pure saving (which guards against immediate shocks) to investment, which means accepting that part of the money moves away for a time and fluctuates in exchange for the chance to grow. Both functions coexist in a mature financial architecture.

There's no ideal instant to start investing, just as there's no perfect day to start going to the gym, but there is one thing about timing that does matter. People who try to enter and exit the market by anticipating ups and downs get, on average, worse results than those who get in and stay. It goes against the legends of the Wall Street wizards, but it's true. Long-term returns come more from the distribution among assets than from timing or instrument selection.[35] That frees us from the burden of having to make a brilliant entrance or force ourselves into memorable acrobatics. The most important thing is to start, once we have a decision framework.

The traditional methods explain first Markowitz's efficient frontier, how Sharpe's CAPM works, what instruments exist, and what returns they've had. Then they run a risk-profile questionnaire with generic questions about reactions to hypothetical drops, and with that superficial information they choose a supposedly optimal portfolio. This is decidedly wrong,

---

[35]Gary P. Brinson, L. Randolph Hood, and Gilbert L. Beebower, "Determinants of Portfolio Performance," Financial Analysts Journal 42, no. 4 (1986): 39–44.

and the flaw is in the order. Starting with technical theory and adding psychology as a cosmetic adjustment is a recipe for disaster. The INVERSO Engine reverses that sequence. As from the beginning, in the terrain of strategy too we'll start with our real coordinates and only afterward work through the technical terrain, in a way that can actually be sustained.

We call it an "Engine" because it takes frequently irregular or imperfect energy and transforms it into a movement that can be sustained over long periods without constant supervision. A well-designed engine produces movement despite our clumsy decisions out of fatigue, panic, or euphoria, and despite the economic contexts we don't control, and that's what we're going to build.

The Coordinate Quadrant

Before choosing a single instrument, we need to know where we're operating from, with the life we actually lead. Across I, N, and V we did deep work of self-knowledge, and now we know our financial signature, which biases dominate us, where our breaking points are, how our budget works, and how much margin we have, like a mountaineer who knows themselves well and knows at what altitude breathing gets hard, how they react to extreme cold, how many days they can hold out without descending, and at what moment they tend to make bad decisions.

All that knowledge is enormous and valuable, but very general. It works for any mountain. Now there's a concrete mountain ahead. We have to invest in a specific market, in a specific country, at this moment of life, and not everything we know about ourselves is equally relevant to this particular climb. The coordinate quadrant is the filter that takes that self-knowledge and translates it into four operational variables for the specific task of investing. It works like the equipment check a mountaineer does before setting out with what's needed for their mountain. It's the Engine's outer gear, and it sets the operating parameters to make sure it works for us and not for a generic investor who doesn't exist.

The professional practice of financial advising has always used three coordinates to locate the investor: what they want to achieve, how much time they have, and how much risk they tolerate. It's what the industry calls an "Investment Policy Statement," the obligatory starting point of any serious strategy, from the big investment funds to the apps that ask us to fill out a "risk profile" in five questions. The two most demanding international certifications in the sector, the CFA for investment management and the CFP for personal financial planning, formalized this scheme in the '80s, and today it's used as the professional standard in more than a hundred and seventy countries. It's the global consensus of an entire industry. In the INVERSO Engine, those coordinates are filled with everything we built in the earlier chapters, and a fourth coordinate is added that powers it up. Let's review each one.

Goals. We already dealt with this in N. We know what we want to achieve and how much return the strategy has to produce to make it possible. What matters now is what each kind of goal demands of the investment, because they don't all ask for the same thing. A modest goal, where the amount needed is reachable with regular contributions and conservative returns, asks for little, and consistency and low cost are enough. We don't need the market to do anything spectacular, so low-risk funds and automatic contributions handle this without drama.

By contrast, an ambitious goal, where the amount needed exceeds what regular contributions can cover on their own, asks for growth, and for that we need the market to work in our favor, which means accepting volatility. This is the moment we accept there's no shortcut. If we expect high returns with no exposure to risk, we're after something that doesn't exist, or worse, trusting someone who tells us it does.

If the goal is critical and failing would have serious consequences, for example, the down payment on a home, certainty has to come above everything. If a goal is critical and ambitious at the same time, there are no fully safe financial instruments, and it's time to extend the timeline or increase contributions, or, of course, reduce the ambition. Believing the market will solve the equation by sheer luck can turn the adventure into a fiasco. Knowing what's at stake behind the goals, we have to treat them as commitments to future versions of ourselves that must be honored by applying the best strategy.

Horizon. The temporal dimension of an investment has at least two faces. One, objective, indicates when we'll need the money. If we're saving for the down payment on a house two years out, the horizon is two years, regardless of how much we'd like to tolerate volatility or aspire to higher returns. Time radically changes the meaning of risk. In the short term, a sharp market drop can be devastating simply because it doesn't give us enough time to recover. In the long term, the logic changes, because over horizons of ten or fifteen years the historical probability that a diversified portfolio of global stocks ends in a loss falls dramatically. Here time is an ally, absorbing part of the volatility along the way.

Risk tolerance. Investment questionnaires usually ask what we'd do if the portfolio lost 20 percent in a year. The answers don't always help, because we respond differently in calm than when we watch our real money fall. In the abstract we're rational, patient, and commited to the long term. In the middle of a crisis we discover our less zen side. Risk tolerance, as we've seen, doesn't come from technical knowledge or intellectual courage. We can understand perfectly that market drops are normal and still spend sleepless nights when they happen, and there's no guilt in that.[36] A strategy we can't sustain emotionally is a bad strategy.

Let's also reckon that tolerance changes enormously over a lifetime. We don't react the same way to volatility after going through an illness, a divorce, spells of unemployment, or anything that shows us the dark side of life. The volatility we used to withstand without trouble can become unbearable, or the dangers

---

[36]John E. Grable, "Financial Risk Tolerance and Additional Factors That Affect Risk Taking in Everyday Money Matters," Journal of Business and Psychology 14, no. 4 (2000): 625–630.

that once seemed threatening can now be met almost with boredom. Someone who has already been through several crises and watched their portfolio recover usually tolerates drops better. Panic gradually loses its power. It becomes something we've seen before and know how to survive. By contrast, someone just starting out can experience a relatively normal dip as if it were the collapse of the world financial system.

In general, people who live through periods of low stock returns are less willing to take financial risk, and if they do, they expose a smaller portion of their money. This happens more when the experience is recent, but if we saw it in childhood it can be indelible. The generation that spent its youth during the '30s invested cautiously the rest of their lives, and they're called "the Depression babies."[37] The German hyperinflation of 1923, which at one point doubled prices every few days and turned paper money into fuel for stoves, still explains, a century later, the anti-inflationary obsession of German economic policy.[38] Chronic instability leaves the same sediment. In Argentina, where the currency lost thirteen zeros since 1970 and deposits were confiscated, that distrust shows up in the culture of dollarizing savings and disbelieving promises of returns in local currency. It sounds very sensible, but rejecting all risk means losing, out of fear, opportunities that are worth it.

Something similar happens, in a less dramatic key, with the moment in the cycle. After years of sustained rises we feel bolder, right when prices are high and the real risk is greater; after a sharp drop, when assets are cheap and history says it's the best time to get in, the same risk seems intolerable and we flee. It's one of the costliest paradoxes of financial behavior: brave when prudence would serve and prudent when courage would.

---

[37]Ulrike Malmendier and Stefan Nagel, "Depression Babies: Do Macroeconomic Experiences Affect Risk-Taking?," The Quarterly Journal of Economics 126, no. 1 (2011): 373–416.

[38]Fabio Braggion, Felix von Meyerinck, and Nic Schaub, "Inflation and Individual Investors' Behavior: Evidence from the German Hyperinflation," The Review of Financial Studies 36, no. 12 (2023): 5012–5045.

Notice that this is the graveyard spiral we began this book with. The disoriented pilot feels they're climbing when they're really falling, and their instinct to pull back on the controls is exactly what tightens the spiral and crashes them. With money it's the same. The visceral feeling of the moment screams at us to buy because everything's going up or to sell before it's too late. Like the pilot, we have to be guided by the instruments, that is, by the structure we designed in cold blood. The INVERSO turn is simple: even in fear or euphoria, we keep our hands on the controls. The financial signature we identified in I tells us our pattern of reaction under pressure, and the identity anchoring of N already showed us when in the cycle and in what form our bias will fire. Here we have to integrate that knowledge into the rest of the strategy.

Available energy. Let's introduce a fourth coordinate into the quadrant, to measure how much real attention we can devote to a financial strategy without destroying other parts of our life. When our cognitive bandwidth is saturated, the ability to decide well deteriorates much faster than we usually admit.[39] The right investment strategy for someone single, with a relaxed job and a genuine interest in finance as a hobby, can be completely absurd for someone holding down exhausting workdays, small children, sick parents, or an emotionally chaotic life. In that context, the last thing we need is to spend hours rebalancing assets. The ideal strategy is the one our concrete life can sustain.

In practice, the level of complexity of the portfolio has to match the energy of the life stage we're in. Back to aviation, managing money isn't flying a small plane on a forty-minute trip, where you stay alert to every instant because the trip is short and you enjoy the scenery. It's more like an intercontinental flight of many hours, almost always with passengers aboard (a partner, children, parents who depend on us) and at an altitude where a mistake is fatal. Pilots aren't on the controls for twelve hours straight. Even less so

---

[39]Mullainathan and Shafir, Scarcity, op. cit.

if the flight repeats, with layovers, for decades. Planes have autopilot so the crew can eat, rest, and handle an emergency with a clear head. A portfolio should work the same way. When energy is high, we can run a more complex strategy that asks for frequent attention, but when low-energy seasons hit us (an illness, a grief, a newborn, a work crisis, or simply interests elsewhere) we need an autopilot. In designing the strategy, we have to ask how long it holds on its own when we can't watch it.

These four coordinates form a system of interlocking constraints. When they align, a zone of strategic coherence emerges, a space where multiple portfolio configurations work, fitting our financial and life goals together.

Every strategy is shaped by the financial identity we explored in I. Two people with identical goals, identical horizon, similar technical tolerance, and comparable available energy may need radically different strategies because their signatures process those coordinates in incompatible ways. But signatures aren't fixed psychological verdicts. They're learned patterns that can change when we accumulate enough experience to question their assumptions. An Accumulator who goes through several market drops and observes sustained recoveries slowly begins to loosen their permanent expectation of catastrophe, and a Controller can learn that intervening less destroys less value than obsessively watching every move. Those transformations require the initial design to be compatible with the real signature. There, finally, the zone of strategic coherence appears, the point where what's technically reasonable coincides with what's psychologically sustainable.

So far we've prepared the engine to drive us without harming us, but those coordinates on their own still don't tell us what to do concretely with the money. They mark out the territory within which a strategy can work without breaking, and they leave us ready to enter the technical territory proper. Now we need to understand the structural rules of the system.

The Technical Territory

Modern financial theory, since Harry Markowitz's work in the 1950s, holds that we can't maximize expected return without taking on risk.[40] We've been insisting on this. It doesn't matter whether we like it, just as gravity doesn't wait for our opinion to keep our feet on the ground. There's a set of optimal portfolios, where each point represents the maximum expected return for a given level of risk. We can't go beyond that "efficient frontier," and all that's left is to choose where to position ourselves. William Sharpe took this further with the Capital Asset Pricing Model, stating that any investment moves along a pole between what we could earn risk-free and the risk we accept by exposing ourselves to the market.[41] Put simply, if we're promised high return with low risk, something is off.

Although no financial engineering can cancel this relationship, an intelligent design knows how much structural risk we tolerate and builds accordingly. But what is risk? Put briefly, it's the possibility of loss that produces uncertainty. Put that way, it seems like something controlled with more prudence, but, as often happens in life, the matter has more twists. In fact, the classic presentation ignores that besides maximizing risk-adjusted return, we seek to minimize the probability of regretting our decisions, and that potential regret modifies the strategies we adopt.[42]

There is, of course, a regret of action that appears when we do something and it goes wrong, for example, when we buy crypto at the peak and lose seventy percent. It hurts because we feel it was our fault. But there's also a regret of omission, which appears when we don't do something that would have been right. For example, we don't buy when it was cheap and then it rises dramatically. The

---

[40] Harry Markowitz, "Portfolio Selection," Journal of Finance 7, no. 1 (1952): 77–91. Markowitz received the Nobel Prize in Economics in 1990 for this work.

[41] William F. Sharpe, "Capital Asset Prices: A Theory of Market Equilibrium under Conditions of Risk," Journal of Finance 19, no. 3 (1964): 425–442.

[42] Meir Statman, Behavioral Finance: The Second Generation (CFA Institute Research Foundation, 2019). See also Meir Statman, "Behavioral Finance versus Standard Finance," in Behavioral Finance and Investment Management (CFA Institute, 2010).

pain is more diffuse than that of the failed action, but just as real. It feels like having missed something everyone else got. But the distinction reveals a trap. On the other side of risk there's discomfort too. If we don't invest out of fear of losing, the slow regret awaits us of watching inflation and missed opportunities erode what was hard to come by. We can bury our head like an ostrich, but it will happen anyway. What if we ask ourselves which kind of discomfort we can manage better? By now we know how to answer: it depends on the signature.

The Optimist tolerates regret of action well but is destroyed by regret of omission. They need some exposure to high-potential assets, because the psychological cost of not being there if they take off is greater than that of being there and losing. The Avoider suffers regret of action but coexists fine with omission. Seeing others win produces no depressive spiral. The Controller lives badly with both and needs a strategy that minimizes the probability of being wrong in any direction. The Accumulator tolerates both poorly, but above all action, because each loss confirms that the world is dangerous. The Compensator has variable tolerance. In emotional expansion they reinterpret loss as experience; in moments of fragility, by contrast, it becomes a devastating verdict. The Protector, for their part, suffers action regret intensely if the results affect the group.

In many cases it makes sense to include "symbolic allocations" of small percentages in high-potential speculative assets, typically between two and five percent of the portfolio, with the primary function of regret management. The marginal loss of efficiency is offset by an enormous gain in psychological sustainability.

Let's return to the question of time, because there's a fascinating debate worth knowing before designing any portfolio. The most widely circulated version says, in a reassuring tone, that if we invest for the long term, risk dilutes. Markets rise more than they fall, returns average out, and time heals all wounds. Jeremy Siegel spent decades documenting this thesis, and the historical data give it a solid base.[43] For horizons of twenty or thirty years, it's genuinely reassuring. Still, it has a catch that Paul Samuelson identified with elegance and a certain mischief. It's true that the annual average stabilizes over the years, but the uncertainty about the total accumulated amount increases.[44] Think of it this way: if we flip a coin ten times, the ratio of heads to tails will be near 50 percent. If we flip it ten thousand times, closer still. But the absolute difference between heads and tails can be enormous.

It's the same with investments. Over twenty years, the average annual return will probably resemble the historical one, but the distance between the best and worst possible scenario of accumulated wealth is much greater than at one year. Time smooths the average but amplifies the range of final outcomes. If we still doubt, there's an even more suggestive fact. If time really eliminated risk, protecting a stock portfolio against losses should get cheaper the longer the horizon. In fact the opposite happens. The insurance costs more, not less. The market, which counts better than we do, doesn't treat the long term as something of lesser risk.[45]

Who's right? Probably both sides, because they're talking about different things. The probability of ending in a loss falls with time. The possible magnitude of that loss, if it happens, rises. For practical life, what matters is that at twenty years the chances of a diversified portfolio losing are historically very low. The second point reminds us that "very low" isn't zero, and that designing as if it were is a form of exaggerated optimism we have to avoid.

Concretely, if we need the money in less than three years, we have to protect it. A market drop six months before buying an

---

[43]Jeremy J. Siegel, Stocks for the Long Run: The Definitive Guide to Financial Market Returns & Long-Term Investment Strategies, 6th ed. (New York: McGraw-Hill, 2022).

[44]Paul A. Samuelson, "Risk and Uncertainty: A Fallacy of Large Numbers," Scientia 98 (1963): 108–113. See also the volumes of Collected Scientific Papers of Paul A. Samuelson (Cambridge, MA: MIT Press, 1966–1986).

[45]Zvi Bodie, "On the Risk of Stocks in the Long Run," Financial Analysts Journal 51, no. 3 (1995): 18–22. See also Zvi Bodie, Alex Kane, and Alan J. Marcus, Investments, 1st ed. (Homewood, IL: Irwin, 1989).

apartment is closer to catastrophe than to an interesting fluctuation. The money has to be in stable instruments, even if they yield little, because we're buying certainty. Between three and ten years, the ground becomes mixed. We need some growth so inflation doesn't eat the effort, but not so much exposure that a crisis two years from the goal forces us to rethink everything. It's the stretch where mixed portfolios of bonds and stocks belong. Beyond ten years, and especially beyond twenty, history is on our side, though without total guarantees. Again, the probability that a diversified portfolio of global stocks ends in a real loss is very low, and the cost of not having been exposed to growth becomes extremely high.

Now, there's a variable the books usually present as a third corner of the triangle alongside risk and return, but it's really something else: liquidity. It isn't on the same conceptual level, because it's something we need depending on our situation and it acts as a constraint on the available options. The less liquid assets, the ones we can't convert into cash quickly, pay a return premium for that inconvenience. It's logical, because no one accepts having money trapped for years unless they're paid for the patience.

Liquidity, however, has two layers that get permanently confused. Financial liquidity measures objectively how long it takes us to turn an investment into cash without losing value in the process. Selling shares of a large company on an active exchange takes seconds; selling an apartment in a midsize city can take months, and if we're in a hurry, at a ferocious discount. Selling a stake in a private business can take years, if we find a buyer at all. So far it's all pure mechanics, but there's another important layer: psychological liquidity, which measures how the impossibility of getting out is experienced. An asset can be technically sellable in weeks at a moderate loss and still generate an oppressive sense of being trapped, like a mountaineer who can technically descend but feels the mountain won't let them go.

Here the signatures reappear. The Avoider, for example, needs high psychological liquidity because the feeling of being shut in triggers their avoidance unbearably. If they feel they can't get out, they'll stop looking and let themselves go. The Controller, by contrast, can tolerate low financial liquidity as long as they have visibility over the process. With the exit in sight, even if it takes time, they relax. The Optimist tolerates low liquidity better than any other profile, because they genuinely don't think about the need for emergency exits, which is an advantage until the day they need one.

The practical rule is to keep in liquid assets, convertible to cash within days without significant loss, at least one year of essential expenses plus any foreseeable large expense in the next two or three years. That liquidity floor works like the last safe camp before the summit, giving us room for the rest of the portfolio to work without every market swing pushing us into premature decisions.

Half-hidden off to one side, there are always silent killers ready to destroy our returns. Costs. Management fees, entry and exit spreads, taxes on gains: all that paraphernalia seems insignificant in an isolated year, but while compound interest grows our money, it also grows what we're charged to manage it. John Bogle devoted his professional life to documenting this phenomenon and showed that a fund charging two percent annual fees can take more than sixty percent of the accumulated gain over a fifty-year horizon.[46] Two-thirds of what the market produced goes to compounded fees. Really. Every percentage point of fees is a percentage point less of return.

Before choosing any instrument, it's worth finding out the total annual cost, the percentage the fund or product charges to manage it. It appears in the documentation under names like TER or expense ratio, depending on the market. The number varies enormously by country and type of instrument. A global ETF on an international platform can charge less than 0.2 percent a year; a

[46]John C. Bogle, "The Arithmetic of 'All-In' Investment Expenses," Financial Analysts Journal 70, no. 1 (2014): 13–21. See also John C. Bogle, The Little Book of Common Sense Investing: The Only Way to Guarantee Your Fair Share of Stock Market Returns (Hoboken, NJ: Wiley, 2007).

local fund in an emerging market can charge ten or twenty times more for a similar product. The rule is to always compare the total cost of what we're about to choose against the cheapest alternative. If the difference isn't justified by a concrete service we can name, we're overpaying. The second number is the transaction cost, how much the platform charges each time we buy or sell. If we operate monthly with automatic contributions, that cost is multiplied by twelve and has to be added to the total. The third is the tax cost in our jurisdiction. Two investments with identical gross return can have radically different net return after taxes. These three numbers, added together, are the real price of our strategy. If the price is too high, we're financing other people's wealth with our own.

And if we have a large sum available? Do we invest it all at once or little by little? The empirical research favors investing everything immediately, because markets rise more often than they fall, and every day out is a day that doesn't capture that growth.[47] Still, if investing it all at once gives us paralyzing anxiety or raises the probability that we sell in panic at the first drop, then the technically optimal strategy is emotionally unworkable. Entering gradually over six or twelve months sacrifices some expected return in exchange for the ability to sustain the strategy, which is what matters most.

4. Instruments, Architectures, and Fit

With the quadrant, the signatures, and the technical picture clear, let's go over the concrete tools and the designs that organize them, to see how all of it connects with the person who'll sustain it for years.

---

[47]Vanguard Research, Dollar-Cost Averaging Just Means Taking Risk Later (Valley Forge, PA: Vanguard Group, 2012).

The Catalog

Let's open the pack and go over the tools one by one. None is magic or good for everything, but fitted to the quadrant we already traced and to the stretch of mountain where they'll operate, they're what we need. Let's look at the categories that cover most people's needs with sensible long-term strategies, from the most defensive to the most exposed.

Let's start with what absolutely goes at the bottom: deposits and low-risk funds. There are few things less exciting in a portfolio, and that's exactly why they're so important. They hold value with minimal risk and maximum liquidity, firm ground beneath everything else. Interest-bearing accounts and certificates of deposit offer rates known in advance with reasonable liquidity and protection through deposit insurance up to certain limits. In stable economies, those rates tend to hover around inflation or fall just below it, so they preserve nominal value while losing a little real purchasing power, which is fine, because their job is simply to keep us from sliding backward. Money market funds go a step further, investing in very short-term instruments of the highest credit quality. They're the sophisticated equivalent of keeping cash under the mattress, but with some yield. They sit there, stable, boring, and utterly reliable on the day we need them because the mountain has turned ugly.

Let's climb a stretch. Bonds are the rope that connects the points of the ascent and lets the rest move safely. A bond is a relatively simple pact where we lend money to a government or a company, they pay us periodic interest, and at the end of the term they return the principal. The apparent simplicity hides a very wide range. The sovereign bonds of stable countries pay modest rates because the risk is tiny, and in moments of global crisis, when everything else collapses, they tend to rise, because frightened investors run to shelter in them. Like a piton set well in the rock, they hold when everything else gives way. The sovereign bonds of volatile countries, by contrast, pay very high rates, and that generosity is a warning that there's a very real risk they won't pay us or will restructure the debt. Corporate bonds are in the middle, and the rate difference from the same country's government bond, what's called the "credit spread," prices the risk of the company going bankrupt. Inflation-linked bonds guarantee real purchasing power instead of nominal values that can evaporate, which in countries with chronic inflation makes them a basic survival tool. For their part, the global bonds of countries with a tradition of paying let us dollarize or internationalize part of the portfolio, a way of not having all the ropes tied to the same anchor. Together, bonds make the portfolio breathe, so that when stocks plunge, the total doesn't fall as much. With this defensive piece, we can take more risk on the offensive ones.

Now the ground tilts. Stocks represent ownership in real companies. When we buy a share, we buy a tiny fraction of a company that exists in the physical world, that makes things, employs people, and can grow spectacularly if it innovates or collapse if it makes clumsy decisions or its competitors overtake it. All of that is reflected in the price, which in the short term can move with a violence that's frightening. Here appears the central paradox of investing in stocks. Terrifying in the short term, surprisingly reliable over the long term. The drama dilutes with time, and this reveals where the real risk lies. Yes, in ourselves. Most people who pick good companies still lose because they sell in panic at the worst moment, typically after a drop and right before the recovery they'll miss by having got off the mountain too fast. The enemy, once again, is vertigo, not height.

Here appears the tool that changed financial mountaineering forever: ETFs. An Exchange Traded Fund replicates a complete market index and lets you take part in hundreds or thousands of companies with a single purchase. An S&P 500 ETF gives us a slice of the five hundred largest companies in the United States; an MSCI World one, of some sixteen hundred companies in twenty-three countries. Instead of betting that we'll guess which of all those companies will win, we keep a piece of all of them at once.

The advantages are instant diversification, very low costs, and emotional simplicity. There's no need to fall in love with any company or suffer the fall of any one in particular, which is worth a great deal. Behind this tool is an idea that earned Eugene Fama the Nobel. If market prices already incorporate all available information, beating the market systematically requires inside information, which is illegal, or a superhuman analytical ability sustained over decades, which is statistically very improbable.[48] ETFs are, at bottom, a peace treaty with that reality: instead of fighting a mountain that knows more than we do, we let it do its work and ride its growth. For the average investor with a complex life and limited energy, it's hard to find something that works so well with so little wear.

Let's talk now about the rock everyone thinks they know: real estate. As the star asset of the financial imagination, it's surrounded by mythology. "Bricks never go down," people say, as if it were a law of physics. Robert Shiller, another Nobel laureate, showed that it isn't so. Housing, once we discount inflation, maintenance, taxes, and all the associated costs, has a real return close to zero over long horizons when looked at on a global scale.[49] There are places and eras where it shoots up, true, but also entire decades of stagnation. This doesn't mean buying your own home is a mistake: it offers a quality of life stability no return can measure: knowing no one will ask you to leave. Still, we shouldn't confuse that value with growth in net worth. Concentrating an enormous portion of net worth in bricks, believing it's the "conservative" option, is really a concentrated bet on a single asset, impossible to sell in parts and slow to sell whole. The famous rental income, sold as "passive income," is rarely so passive. There are tenants, vacancies, two-in-the-morning breakdowns, and constant decisions. For

---

48Eugene F. Fama, "Efficient Capital Markets: A Review of Theory and Empirical Work," Journal of Finance 25, no. 2 (1970): 383–417. Fama received the Nobel Prize in Economics in 2013.

49Robert J. Shiller, Irrational Exuberance, 3rd ed. (Princeton, NJ: Princeton University Press, 2015). Shiller received the Nobel Prize in Economics in 2013, in part for his work on asset bubbles.

those who want to invest in the sector without becoming an on-call plumber, there are REITs, which trade like stocks, sell in seconds, and diversify across many properties, though in exchange for moving with the market's volatility. Real estate has its place in a diversified portfolio because it doesn't move at the same rhythm as stocks and bonds and protects directly against inflation, but it's one piece of the gear, never the whole pack.

Here we reach the hotly disputed territory of cryptocurrencies. It's worth starting by recognizing that they emerged as a response to real problems: uncontrolled money printing that dilutes savings, intermediaries who charge dearly and can cut off access, fragile centralized systems, and the exclusion of billions who don't even have a bank account. Bitcoin was designed as a digital store of value, with a supply limited to twenty-one million units, which makes it resistant to inflation by design and hard to confiscate. Ethereum, by contrast, aims to be the infrastructure for contracts and financial systems that run without intermediaries. The problems they try to solve are genuine, even if the solutions drag their own ghosts. Their volatility can split a fortune in half in weeks; the technical complexity opens the door to costly mistakes; regulation shifts from country to country; and the ecosystem is riddled with genuinely bizarre scams. Like the steepest, least mapped face of the mountain, it can offer wonderful views, but it's not a place for beginners or for taking the whole tent. The reasonable rule is moderate exposure, between 2 percent and 10 percent of the portfolio, acknowledging the potential without staking everything on it, and always after the base camp is well set up. Never before.

On the other side of time is the oldest asset of all: gold. It has been a store of value for thousands of years and has survived the fall of empires, world wars, hyperinflations that turned paper money into painted paper, and the complete replacement of one monetary system by another. Remarkable. Now, gold preserves purchasing power over very long periods without increasing it. If an ancestor of ours had bought gold a century ago, today we could buy more or less the same as they could, no more and no less, though we'd have come through all the catastrophes of the road intact.[50] Gold keeps its value precisely because it doesn't depend on any government that has to pay its debt or any bank with solvency problems to go on being gold. It goes in the portfolio in small doses, between 2 percent and 10 percent, like that thermal blanket that takes up little space in the pack and on the day of the storm can save us, but no one climbs a mountain carrying only thermal blankets.

It's also worth thinking of gold and Bitcoin as a pair, because they protect against different dangers. Gold covers the classic risks: war and generalized collapse. Bitcoin covers the contemporary ones gold couldn't anticipate: the over-issuance of currencies, the fragility of hyper-mediated systems. Since we don't know which scenario is more likely, covering both with small exposures makes sense, like someone carrying gear for the snowstorm and for the rainstorm without knowing which will come. The two combined should rarely exceed ten percent of the portfolio, because at bottom they're insurance.

Finally, beyond the standard gear, there's a whole market of alternative investments like real-estate crowdfunding, crowdlending, royalties on creative works, intellectual-property tokenization, thematic innovation indexes, and many others. They're exotic routes. Some can have a place in specific portfolios and for people who understand exactly what they're getting into, but they shouldn't be central pieces for someone with a busy life, which is almost everyone. If we bring them in, let it be in a small fraction and because they genuinely add something we need, not because they sound exciting or came up at dinner. Emotion is a bad adviser on the mountain and worse in investing.

---

[50] Claude B. Erb and Campbell R. Harvey, "The Golden Dilemma," Financial Analysts Journal 69, no. 4 (2013): 10–42.

Three Architectures

Loose tools are useless until they combine into a coherent design, just as a rope and a pair of crampons are only a pile of gear until someone decides how and when to use each thing. Over time, a handful of portfolio architectures have proven themselves, and we'll look at three, ordered from the most sober to the most demanding: the Minimalist, the Balanced, and the Advanced with Multipliers. None is better in the abstract, until we know which fits the coordinate quadrant and the financial signature we have at a given moment of life, which probably isn't the same one we'll have in ten years.

The Minimalist route starts from an indelible principle: life should always be more complex than the portfolio, never the other way around. Minimalism sounds like a small thing, but we don't choose it for lack of resources. On the contrary, it represents the conviction, backed by the evidence, that simplicity well sustained almost always beats improvised sophistication. The mountaineer who knows that each extra piece of gear is one more gram of weight and one more thing that can fail surely chooses this path, which rests on two main pillars and a buffer: around 70 percent in a single diversified global ETF that captures thousands of companies from the developed and emerging world at once; 20 percent in stable government bonds of countries with a solid record of paying; and 10 percent split between gold and crypto for extreme scenarios. That's all. And it's not little. When Vanguard compared simple two- or three-fund portfolios against complex ones with dozens of positions, the simple ones did better, because transaction costs, fees, and the mistakes that come from too many decisions eat away, year after year, any theoretical advantage of complexity.[51] Fewer pieces, fewer things that break, more summit.

The Balanced route starts from a humble premise about our ability to anticipate. The world is large and terribly unpredictable,

---

[51]Vanguard Research, The Case for Low-Cost Index-Fund Investing (Valley Forge, PA: Vanguard Group, 2019).

so instead of betting on knowing what will work, we spread the weight across different regions and economic natures, trusting that when one part stumbles, another is advancing. It assigns 40 percent to global stocks of developed markets, the stable core; 20 percent to emerging markets or innovative sectors, where the fastest and most volatile growth is; 20 percent to quality sovereign and corporate bonds as a defensive counterweight; 10 percent to real estate via REITs, which move at their own rhythm; and two portions of 5 percent in gold and crypto for the storms. It's a solid route, wide and hard to break, because it doesn't depend on any one thing turning out well. If one section of the mountain is impassable, there are others to keep climbing.

The Advanced with Multipliers route is the steep face, ideal for those who want to bet on the future pace of the global economy without falling into pure speculation. It keeps 50 percent in broad global stocks as an anchor, insurance that if we're wrong about everything else, the core keeps stride with the planet's growth; 20 percent in forward-looking sectors such as artificial intelligence, biotechnology, clean energy, or cybersecurity; 10 percent in emerging markets; 10 percent in quality bonds as an internal stabilizer; and 5 percent in gold plus 5 percent in crypto. This route can offer prospects the others don't, beating the traditional indexes by wide margins, but it demands a long horizon of more than ten years and the stomach to watch the portfolio fall, in a bad year, twice as much as the Balanced route without panicking or turning around. If we don't have emotional acclimatization, we can have a rough time.

The Fit

We have the routes now, but we still have to decide which is ours. Let's return to the financial signatures we identified in I, because they, more than any technical calculation, determine which design we'll actually be able to sustain when it snows on the mountain. The fit is the moment when all the work we did converges. The signature of I, the goals of N, the visibility of V, and the coordinate quadrant of E cross to point out, among the possible routes, the one we'll actually be able to walk.

The Accumulator tends to be comfortable on the Minimalist route and had better stay there even if they feel they could do more. They have ambition and the capacity to understand that technically they'd tolerate more volatility, but their real priority is serenity. Every market swing trips their alarm system and consumes energy in anxious watchfulness. They need low noise and spaced-out reviews with a generous emergency cushion that lets them sleep easy. With the years and some positive experience, their signature can mature and allow a gradual migration toward the Balanced route, but that move has to come from them, when they feel ready, never because someone tells them they're being too cautious. An Accumulator pushed onto a more aggressive route than they tolerate will probably bolt.

The Compensator can walk the Minimalist or the Balanced, but in their case what's decisive is how they implement it. They need a system that doesn't demand frequent decisions, because each decision made under emotional stress is a chance for error, and the Compensator makes their worst decisions exactly when the mountain bears down. The automation has to be thorough: automatic monthly contributions, scheduled rebalancing, and above all, frictions that brake the impulse to sell at the worst moment. Those frictions can be technical (a platform that takes days to process a withdrawal), procedural (having to call an adviser and wait forty-eight hours), or social (committing to consult someone trusted before acting). Whatever it is. Any of them amounts to the rope that ties us to a partner. It's there because on the wall, exhausted and afraid, anyone can take a false step.

The Avoider needs the most radical version of the Minimalist route, the simplest humanly possible, with total automation and a structure that lets them forget about it for months or years without anything serious happening. A single global ETF with automatic contributions debited from the bank account serves them infinitely better than any Balanced design of five instruments with quarterly review, because the Avoider won't do the review or the rebalancing. They'll simply put it off, then feel guilty for putting it off, and the guilt will feed more avoidance until they end up abandoning everything. Simplicity is a condition of survival. If over time they develop real interest, they can try sustaining the Minimalist first until the anxiety and avoidance dissolve, and only then weigh whether to add complexity. Always calmly, so it doesn't overwhelm them.

The Controller is the paradox of the group. They have cognitive capacity to spare for the Balanced or even the Advanced route, for understanding complex instruments and processing sophisticated information. Their problem, strictly, is excess, because once they understand something, they can't stop monitoring it. If they choose the Advanced route with thematic sectors, they'll end up spending hours a week reading biotechnology reports and analyzing artificial-intelligence trends, until they're worn out. Paradoxically, they usually need a simpler design than they could technically sustain, with explicit rules for each situation that spare them permanent discretionary judgment. The technical optimization almost never offsets the cost of the exhaustion it generates. They'd do well to repeat, like a mantra, that the summit isn't won by checking the GPS every five minutes.

The Optimist can sustain the Advanced route or the Balanced with a growth tilt. In fact they enjoy it. They tolerate volatility very well, and thinking about the future energizes rather than distresses them. But we already know their Achilles' heel: they assume everything will turn out well when statistically it usually doesn't. The right fit combines a technically ambitious design with firm external limits: scenarios that explicitly account for failure, maximum caps on speculative exposure set in advance, and projections based on the cash flow they actually have, never on uncertain future income. The Optimist is the mountaineer capable of climbing the great summits and posting glorious photos, but also the one who dies on the descent for having spent everything on the way up, convinced that coming down would be easy. They must never forget the railings that keep them on the route.

The Protector can choose the Minimalist or the Balanced, but with two non-negotiable conditions: enough liquidity to be able to help others without dismantling the main portfolio, and a separate rescue fund, with a clear limit defined in advance, meant for exactly that. Without that structure, the Protector will dismantle their own investment every time someone close needs help or they want to support some project, because for them others' need and their place in the group weigh more than their abstract future. They can sustain a more aggressive design as long as liquidity is guaranteed, but any scheme with assets locked up for years is unworkable for them, because they know that when someone needs them, or when they can shine with their contribution, they won't hold back. They'll break whatever stands in the way. Designing with that certainty in mind is pure strategy.

Let's repeat once more that signatures aren't sentences. The INVERSO Method doesn't treat psychological patterns as fixed traits that define us forever; it invites us to recognize and make peace with the design our mind can sustain today, knowing that tomorrow may open paths that look out of reach now.

5. Firing Up the Engine

Everything we've been doing, from understanding portfolio philosophy to matching signature with route, to mapping each architecture's traits, is intellectual worklectual work that happens in calm, sitting with a coffee while life cooperates. Beginning the climb and sustaining the ascent happen in the middle of real life: work bearing down, kids who won't sleep, an unexpectedly high bill, and news of market collapse. The mountain on the map on the wall at home looks little like the one we see while hanging off it in the wind. What follows translates the plan into the first concrete steps, preparing us to sustain them when the weather changes.

First, separate what isn't invested. Before putting a dollar into the market, we have to do the inverse operation and identify the money that stays at base camp, outside every move. The emergency fund, the foreseeable expenses of the coming year, and the committed installments aren't touched. Investing requires capital that can wait, fluctuate, and pass through periods of decline without becoming a daily disaster. If we go up the wall with the money we need to live on, the first storm will force us down at the worst moment, because we have no choice.

The second step is to choose a platform that bores you. The start isn't the moment to show off technical skill. We need a regulated platform where the money is protected by deposit insurance, with a clear interface that lets us understand what we're buying. More than that, let's choose a design that doesn't invite us to look or trade all the time. Many platforms, far from neutral, bombard us with notifications about every market move and comparisons with other investors that breed envy, so we trade more and pay more fees. Others, however, cultivate a healthy boredom. Vanguard did this for decades because entertainment is the enemy of results, and it designed a user experience almost archaic in its simplicity. If the platform entertains us, we're trading too much. A platform that bores us is, in truth, a platform that protects us.

Third, we have to recognize where we operate from. Every strategy is conceived in universal categorie but executed from a concrete place: a country, a currency, a legal system, a financial culture.ure. Switzerland isn't the same as Bolivia, even if the principles are formally identical. Chronic inflation, capital controls, regulatory instability, and access to global markets all condition which instruments are viable. Before choosing them, it's worth asking where the greatest source of uncertainty lies. If the answer points to the country, cross-border diversification is the logical decision, so as not to pitch all the camps on the same unstable slope.

The fourth step is to start with an amount that teaches. The first money we invest serves a function more pedagogical than financial. It shows us how we really react when a number representing our money drops ten percent on a Tuesday morning. If the first drop gives us too much anxiety, the amount is excessive for this phase. If it doesn't even spark curiosity, we won't learn anything. The teaching amount is an investment in self-knowledge: it shows what happens when things get hard and how much energy watching the numbers consumes. Like the acclimatization hike before the ascent, it has us climb a little, come down, and observe how the body responded to the altitude. With that information we'll calibrate the definitive route much better.

The fifth step is to set the rhythm and protect it. Most people obsess over the instruments and neglect the regularity of the contributions. Investing at a clear, predefined frequency turns an isolated decision into a system. Setting up an automatic monthly transfer from the account to the portfolio eliminates hundreds of failed micro-decisions. As an added advantage, it automatically implements a strategy known as dollar-cost averaging. By investing a fixed sum at regular intervals, we buy more units when prices are low and fewer when they're high, reducing the risk of concentrating the whole investment at an unfavorable moment without needing to anticipate market moves.[52] Contributing a little every month for years builds more than a large one-time contribution followed by neglect, just as the short, steady step climbs higher than the heroic start that leaves us gasping within half an hour.

52George M. Constantinides, "A Note on the Suboptimality of Dollar-Cost Averaging as an Investment Policy," Journal of Financial and Quantitative Analysis 14, no. 2 (1979): 443–450. Although technically suboptimal relative to lump-sum investing, dollar-cost averaging reduces perceived volatility and increases the probability that the investor will sustain the strategy, which in practice offsets the theoretical difference.

Finally, the hardest part: learning to do nothing. During the first months, and really during the first years, the greatest risk is intervening. Switching strategy after three months, selling because of an alarming headline, or rotating instruments because someone at dinner mentioned something that's "going up a lot" destroys more value than any correction. Research on investor behavior shows, year after year, that there's a persistent gap between the return the market offers and the one investors actually get, and that gap is largely explained by timing decisions: getting in late and out early, driven by emotions that disguise themselves as analysis.[53] Let's avoid the accident on the descent, when the euphoria of having arrived loosens our attention right on the stretch where it's needed most.

Here the INVERSO Engine reveals its deepest meaning. We call it an engine precisely because it's designed to run on its own. It takes irreIt takes irregular energy (income that rises and falls, attention that comes and goes, mood that fluctuates with life) and converts it into sustained movement into sustained movement without requiring someone to be pushing all the time. Everything we built in this chapter (the separation of capital, the boring platform, the automatic rhythm of contributions, the design fitted to the signature) had the single aim of letting the system advance even when we, on a bad day, want to stop it. "Doing nothing," in this sense, is trusting a mechanism we designed carefully, in a state of calm, to protect us in the moments when we're in no condition to decide.

* * *

A strategy can be flawless on paper and come apart the moment it touches real life. Much as it pains us, decisions about money are

---

[53]The phenomenon is known as the behavior gap. Morningstar documents it with conservative methodology in its annual report Mind the Gap: A Report on Investor Returns (Chicago: Morningstar, 2023).

almost never made at the ideal moment. They're made in the middle of couple fights or right when something we thought was solid collapsed. There the same old impulses return, the ones that know nothing of plans. The mistake is thinking those are exceptions, when it's the normal weather of the mountain. Up to here we've assembled the climbing plan, read the terrain, and deployed our forces, but an expedition is judged by whether everyone comes back. What decides that is what happens when the weather turns foul at four thousand meters. That's what R, Risks, deals with. We're going to look at the design on the day it gets complicated, which is, sooner or later, almost any day.

R

Risks Beyond Numbers

The most dangerous illusion in behavioral finance is believing that knowing about cognitive biases saves us from them, or that recognizing our own financial signature makes it less compulsive. Even the best-designed architecture fractures, at moments, pulled apart by the gap between what we know and what we do, throwing overboard in days what took years to build. This chapter builds on everything we've said about identity and biases and examines the five most destructive emotional events, so we can recognize their anatomy, spot the warning signs, and use protocols to protect ourselves.

1. The Five High-Risk Emotional Events

Some events cause discomfort but are manageable, while others can drag everything doThe list could be long: human life is full of challenges, and no catalogue could exhaust them.could exhaust them. Still, what follows accounts for most of the collapses we see in practice.

Acute personal crises

Severe personal crises affect decision-making and create the need to regain control over something. Anything. The investment portfolio thus becomes the perfect scapegoat. A divorce, for example, can turn into an economic war where what was designed for long-term goals gets torn apart, as a symbol of everything that went wrong. The impulse to liquidate everything and "start from zero" with nothing shared with the other person can be financially devastating. The decisioThe decisions aim to end the pain as fast as possible, at the cost of a future that still feels abstract against the rawness of present grief.present grief. To complicate things, supposedly "fair" divisions according to criteria unrelated to finance often lead to accepting objectively bad agreements.

The future is equally in question in grief, where two simultaneous and contradictory impulses frequently appear. On one side, the impulse to liquidate everything because "nothing matters anymore." Money seems obscene when we've just lost someone irreplaceable, and managing investments seems trivial against the void. On the other, the impulse to do something big and immediate with the money, some gesture that honors the one who died and turns pain into visible action, tends to grow strong. Both have a deep emotional logic. Still, when grief matures, they can come to look like mistakes impossible to undo.

Similarly, a serious illness, especially with a recent diagnosis and uncertain prognosis, collapses the horizon. The portfolio meant for twenty years stops making sense in its original form. Adjusting the strategy for a shorter horizon is fine, but without panicking and dismantling everything at once, especially because most serious illnesses have a trajectory of months or years where partial, staggered liquidity is needed. It's also common for a temptation to emerge: taking disproportionate risks or making desperate investments in extremely expensive alternative therapies. Anything that promises hope. The portfolio becomes a source of financing for that desperation and can be destroyed in weeks. In these cases it's clear that money isn't the priority, but life is hard, and going through an illness without money is even worse than going through it with money, so part of our strength of spirit has to lie in not making mistakes that leave us even more vulnerable.

Without that severity, job loss combines a real need for liquidity with panic, which often overestimates that need. Everything seems insufficient and threatening, and in that state liquidating investments "just in case" seems logical, even when there's an emergency cushion that technically covers months. And beyond being premature, the liquidation may happen at a bad moment, crystallizing losses the design could have absorbed, if only we'd used the emergency cushion for what it was built for:built for: precisely these situations.

Collective euphoria

Speculative bubbles have been studied at least since the Dutch tulip in 1637, when some rare bulbs reached extraordinary prices and became the object of intense speculation. Since then the assets have changed, from tulips to stocks, real estate, dot-com companies, or cryptocurrencies, but the logic remains the conviction that there will always be someone willing to pay more. Lately the keys to interpreting this phenomenon have shifted. Robert Shiller, who received the Nobel Prize in Economics in 2013 in part for his work on asset bubbles, describes them as social and narrative phenomena where the stories that sustained those numbers become temporarily more convincing than reality.[54] The defining feature of a bubble is the growing dissociation between value and price, supported by an increasingly elaborate collective narrative about why "this time is different," usually validated with success stories of people who got rich quickly. They're dangerous for the obvious reason that they collapse, but also because they exert psychological pressure that's hard to resist. When there's a bubble and we decide to sit it out, the social consensus says we're missing a historic opportunity out of cowardice and ignorance.

---

[54]See Robert J. Shiller, Irrational Exuberance, 3rd ed. (Princeton, NJ: Princeton University Press, 2015); idem, Narrative Economics: How Stories Go Viral and Drive Major Economic Events (Princeton, NJ: Princeton University Press, 2019); and idem, "Narrative Economics," American Economic Review 107, no. 4 (2017): 967–1004.

We already talked about regret of omission, which appears when the train has left and we feel we should have gotten on. Here we're interested in a close relative: FOMOFOMO, fear of missing out: the anticipated dread of being left behind, a generalized sense that others are having experiences we're excluded from, typically correlated with dissatisfaction and compulsive [55]social-media use.from, typically correlated with dissatisfaction and compulsive social-media use. In the context of financial bubbles, FOMO is in its element. Stories of spectacular success pour in, and in a situation of uncertainty we look more at what others are doing before deciding. The overabundance of information confirms the bullish narrative, and there's social rejection of anyone who expresses skepticism. As the bubble advances and more people take part with no visible negative consequences, the sense of what's risky gets lost.

The asymmetry between the pain of the falls and the pain of FOMO during bubbles plays an important role. If the fall happens to everyone, it's a shared misfortune, while not taking part means social isolation. Choosing the misfortune of the many sometimes hurts less than being left alone, and we prefer to recover from the blow than to go through the long, unbearable feeling of watching from outside.

Every bubble has a particular narrative that sustains it. In hindsight it can seem absurd, but in the moment it sounds convincing even to intelligent and sophisticated people. In the dot-com bubble, between 1995 and 2000, it was said the internet would transform the economy, which was true, and that therefore the traditional valuation metrics no longer applied, which wasn't. Thus stratospheric valuations of companies with no earnings were justified by arguing they were "capturing market share" in markets that were going to explode. In the U.S. real-estate bubble of 2003–2007, the refrain was that real-estate prices never fell at the

[55]Andrew K. Przybylski et al., "Motivational, Emotional, and Behavioral Correlates of Fear of Missing Out," Computers in Human Behavior 29, no. 4 (2013): 1841–1848.

national level, which was historically true, and that financial innovation through securitization had eliminated risk by distributing it. "This time is different because we understand risk better" was the phrase that preceded the most severe collapse in decades. In the cryptocurrency bubble the stories kept mutating over time. Between 2017 and 2021 it went from the promise that blockchain would completely transform the financial system to the idea that Bitcoin, thanks to its limited supply, would work as a refuge against the inflation and monetary expansion after the pandemic. The unsettling thing is that each narrative contained enough truth to be persuasive, but none of it justified the lunatic valuations.

Telling a bubble from a legitimate opportunity in real time is hard, because both feature rapid price growth, generalized enthusiasm, and narratives about structural change. Still, there are signs that repeat in the historical bubbles, and if they appear, it's worth opening our eyes.

The first thing usually seen is an exponential acceleration of prices. Real opportunities typically have sustained linear or logarithmic growth when looked at over long periods. Bubbles, by contrast, rise faster and faster as they near the peak. We can also notice the growing disconnect between price and historical averages. This doesn't mean everything will collapse tomorrow, but the risk of sudden collapse grows when this happens. Also telling is the change in the profile of participants. Late-stage bubbles draw in masses of people with no prior experience, who frequently go into debt to take part. As the saying goes, when cab drivers give us stock tips, there's a mature bubble. In that increasingly crazed climate, ever more complex instruments proliferate, including crypto, derivative tokens, NFTs of NFTs.Ts. When the instruments become incomprehensible even to veterans of the field, hold on tight. The perfect storm arrives when confidence in the exception circulates. The idea that "this time is different" appears before every major financial crisis of the last eight hundred years.[56] Careful.

The anti-bubble protocol should aim at a deliberate marginal participation that lets us be present without the eventual collapse destroying our entire architecture. The exposure shouldn't exceed 5–10 percent of the portfolio, so that if it collapses it produces absorbable losses. But watch a point that's easy to overlook: that percentage doesn't add to what we already allotted to other assets of the same family. If before we set aside, say, 10 percent for gold and crypto as a hedge, this asset doesn't open a new 5–10 percent on top of that; it competes for the same space. All speculative and hedge assets (gold, Bitcoin, this bet, and any other high-risk one) share a single risk budget within the 100 percent of the portfolio.

The practical rule is to set first a total ceiling for everything volatile together, for example 10 or 15 percent of the portfolio, and only afterward distribute that ceiling among the candidates. What protects the portfolio is the limit on the sum of all of them, not the limit on each asset in isolation. Otherwise, adding up "reasonable" percentages one by one, we'd end up with a quarter of our net worth in assets that can plunge at the same time, which is precisely what these limits aim to avoid. The participation has to come out of the speculative portion of the design, never out of the core of global stocks and bonds that sustain stability.

Above all, let's adopt a mechanical exit rule decided in cold blood. Obviously, we should never go into debt to take part in bubbles. This rule has no exceptions. Finally, it's smart to consolidate the gains from bubbles by integrating them into the conservative core, in the manner of a stroke of luck that probably won't repeat. If it happens, we celebrate; if not, we thank our past self for not having gotten carried away.

---

[56] Carmen M. Reinhart and Kenneth S. Rogoff, This Time Is Different: Eight Centuries of Financial Folly (Princeton, NJ: Princeton University Press, 2009).

Severe market crises

A normal market correction is different from a systemic crisis, though that difference frequently isn't visible until it's late. Corrections are paCorrections are part of the normal functioning of healthy markets, statistical noise absorbed over time.me. Severe crises, by contrast, are events that test the strategy and our ability to keep our faith in the system. In an ordinary downturn, one sector or region stumbles and the weakness spreads gradually; in a systemic crisis, the contagion is nearly instantaneous across widely different assets and geographies. For example, in 2008 the crisis began in U.S. subprime mortgages and within weeks had reached European banks, Asian markets, and commodities.

In normal corrections, even falling assets remain sellable; during general crises there are no buyers at any price. When confidence in the ability to pay is erased, liquidity vanishes, large-scale interventions by central banks and governments become necessary, banks are bailed out, monetary expansion turns extreme, and the normal rules of the market are suspended. If there are bailouts, nothing is normal, and the narrative of breakdowns and collapses drags toward the self-fulfilling prophecy of bank runs and panic selling. We should never underestimate the psychological effect of these market crises, especially because we find it hard to remember and correctly anticipate how intense emotional states feel when we're not in them.[57] In calm moments we have no access to the feeling of panic, and in panic we can't picture the calm certainty that the madness will pass. So each crisis feels unique and terminal while we're inside it.

Let's add the so-called "recency effect," widely studied in cognitive psychology and behavioral finance, according to which the most recent events get disproportionate weight in our probability estimates.[58] The avalanche of negative information

---

[57] George Loewenstein, "Hot-Cold Empathy Gaps and Medical Decision Making," Health Psychology 24, no. 4 (2005).

[58] Amos Tversky and Daniel Kahneman, "Availability: A Heuristic for Judging Frequency and Probability," Cognitive Psychology 5, no. 2 (1973): 207–232. See also

typical of crises buries us in adverse scenarios and keeps us from picturing longer horizons, even when the historical data don't necessarily justify that extreme level of pessimism. Those catastrophic accounts are also overwhelming: we can imagine banks failing, cwe can imagine banks failing, chaos in the streets, prolonged depression, but not the technical mechanisms of recovery involving complex monetary policy and international coordination.y and international coordination.

This combination is seen, for example, in the 2008 crisis. Ben Bernanke, chair of the Fed, in his Jackson Hole speech, stated that there were moments during those weeks when he wasn't sure the banking system would keep functioning.[59] In the 2020 pandemic, the S&P 500 fell 35 percent in roughly a month, the fastest drop in modern history, driven by deep uncertainty about timelines and consequences. The market's recovery within months, propelled by the massive intervention of central banks and by the development of vaccines faster than anticipated, wasn't predictable in March 2020.

As a protocol, it's worth having simple, mechanical rules executable under panic, especially the one to continue with the planned course, including contributions and rebalancing. Only three situations justify modifying the portfolio: a genuine liquidity need when the emergency cushion is exhausted, a life event independent of the crisis, or the design becoming psychologically unsustainable. Only those three. Never because we lost money or everyone is selling. If anxiety eats at us, let's opt for less exposure to the news to get through the tension of the moment. Let's remember all of this is a narrative effect. There's one additional reason to act, but it touches only those who have debts. It may be

---

Ulrike Malmendier, "Experience Effects in Finance: Foundations, Applications, and Future Directions," Review of Finance 25, no. 5 (2021); and Nihat Cakici et al., "Recency Bias and the Cross-Section of International Stock Returns," Journal of International Financial Markets, Institutions and Money 84 (2023).

[59]Ben S. Bernanke, "Reflections on a Year of Crisis," speech at the Federal Reserve Bank of Kansas City's Annual Economic Symposium, Jackson Hole, Wyoming, BIS Review 27 (2009).

worth deleveraging quickly so as not to be trapped with large positions financed by loans that can explode when the market turns ugly. Nothing more.

And the crisis as opportunity? Buying at these moments is a real opportunity, but only with capital we don't need. Warren Buffett, the Oracle of Omaha, made the line famous: "Be fearful when others are greedy and greedy when others are fearful."[60] It sounds good and is statistically correct, but it turns out to be extremely hard to do. Holding what we have and buying small additional amounts isn't a bad idea.

Unexpected success and sudden money

Paradoxically, receiving a large sum of unexpected money is often more financially destructive than not receiving it, because sudden money shuts down the normal circuits of prudence and activates processing circuits poorly calibrated for long-term decisions. The case of lottery winners is classic. Between 70 and 75 percent, regardless of educational level and prior economic situation, end up in a worse financial situation five years after winning. Why? We usually order money mentally according to its origin, and "free" money (from inheritances, bonuses, settlements, or speculative gains) feels more available for spending than money earned through regular work, even though both are worth exactly the [61]same.

This sets off several connected mechanisms. Effort disconnects from reward, and the money is spent lightly because it doesn't feel hard-earned. We suddenly decree that it's time to enjoy, sometimes to the point of spending it all and even going into debt, prisoners of the illusion of permanent wealth. Gains feel like absolute

---

[60]Warren E. Buffett, "Letter to Shareholders," 2004 Annual Report (Berkshire Hathaway Inc., 2005).

[61]Richard Thaler, "Mental Accounting and Consumer Choice," Marketing Science 4, no. 3 (2005).

[62]transformations. A million dollars all at once feels like an enormous change, even if it can't fully alter the trajectory of someone who needs to sustain expenses for decades. Still, the subjective sense of transformative wealth overwhelms us. If we add the social pressure of those who expect us to share the "luck," the chaos that ends in the loss of life structure is created.

Spending nothing in the first six months, time enough for the euphoria to subside, for the money to start feeling normal, and for us to assess requests from those close to us with more distance, is a very good option.ion. If we have no experience handling large sums, professional consultation is mandatory, since it lets us add the perspective of someone with no direct emotional interest before making decisions. On the other hand, we'd do well to integrate a significant part of the sudden money, ideally between 60 and 75 percent, into the long-term design as if it were savings accumulated gradually. Instead of spending it on expenses or "opportunities" or lending it to relatives, we invest it in the long-term portfolio. The rest can be used for things that improve our quality of life, for example, eliminating expensive debt or home improvements.

Setting a budget for generosity is useful: it lets us give with clear criteria and stop without guilt when the budget runs out. Sudden money also isn't used to take on permanent or very long-term commitments. For example, you don't buy a house significantly more expensive than the current one with permanent maintenance costs. Let's also rule out promises of indefinite financial support to relatives, or taking on bor taking on business partners with no clear exit, commitments that generate expectations others will eventually find impossible to sustain. impossible to sustain.

---

[62]Daniel Kahneman and Amos Tversky, "Prospect Theory: An Analysis of Decision under Risk," Econometrica 47, no. 2 (1979). See also Nicholas C. Barberis, "Thirty Years of Prospect Theory in Economics: A Review and Assessment," Journal of Economic Perspectives 27, no. 1 (2013): 173–196; and Michaela Pagel, "Expectations-Based Reference-Dependent Life-Cycle Consumption," The Review of Economic Studies 84, no. 2 (2017): 885–934.

Big life changes should happen after the trial period where we experience what it's like to live with less regular income and more free time. Many people discover that what they imagined wanting when they had sudden money isn't really what they wanted, but by then it's too late to undo the changes.

Prolonged exhaustion

Burnout or extreme exhaustion is a much-underestimated emotional risk in personal finance, because it doesn't depend on the market or on external economic events. Still, whatever its cause, the saturation from the gradual wearing-down of cognitive and emotional resources eventually collapses our ability to make any decision, including financial ones. As a result, capacities like planning, evaluating future consequences, and holding multiple considerations at once deteriorate sharply.

During burnout there's usually a powerful impulse to reduce fronts in order to lower the overload. Strictly speaking, well-designed investments aren't a real source of cognitive load, but they seem to be because they involve money, which always feels problematic. Real simplification under burnout means keeping systems that run automatically and cutting activities that require frequent decisions. A well-designed portfolio with automatic contributions and scheduled rebalancing requires minimal attention, and liquidating it, on the contrary, increases cognitive load because now you have to decide what to do with the cash and when to reinvest, all while we lose potential growth.

Those destructive actions under burnout disguise themselves as prudence and maturity, but they miss the target. The complexity that overwhelms us usually comes from other areas of life (work, relationships, caretaking, health problems), but since those are hard or impossible to change quickly,e to change quickly, we reach for the portfolio, which can be changed in minutes, to feel we're regaining some control. In these cases, as in others we've seen, it's worth protecting what we've gained by putting the portfolio in pure automatic mode with no review. It's literally worth making our own access to investment accounts difficult. That, of course, doesn't mean blocking them completely, but deleting apps from the phone or canceling notifications are part of effective emergency hygiene.

In these extreme circumstances the impulses are typically momentary, so ten or fifteen minutes can make the difference. Faced with an overwhelming impulse to simplify, it usually works to design it in writing without executing it, like someone writing a resignation letter when furious but not sending it. The act of writing relieves, and when the acute state passes we can review whether we really want to resign. The example isn't accidental. The temptation to quit jobs in these situations is powerful, but we should never put at risk the income sufficient to cover essential expenses without touching investments. Mental health is serious, and professional help is worth seeking when needed. In the meantime, a good protocol helps direct action quickly without destroying accumulated effort along the way, through safeguards designed to keep temporary crises from becoming permanent damage.

Ulysses tying himself to the mast so he could hear the sirens without losing his mind is a powerful example. Ulysses understands that, under the influence of the song of those marvelous beings, his willpower will falter and even turn against him, and that's why he asks to be bound to the mast to limit the reach of his impulses. Jon Elster used this metaphor to illustrate precommitment, that is, the resource of anticipating a future weakness and restricting our options to protect the long term.[63] This intuition has a direct precedent in the idea of strategic commitment, according to which voluntarily limiting one's own future freedom can be rational when there's a conflict of interest, even within the same individual.[64] More recently this line of

---

[63]Jon Elster, Ulysses and the Sirens: Studies in Rationality and Irrationality (Cambridge: Cambridge University Press, 1979).

[64]Thomas C. Schelling, The Strategy of Conflict (Cambridge, MA: Harvard University Press, 1960); Micromotives and Macrobehavior (New York: W. W. Norton, 1978); and

thinking fed research on spending limits, apps that block digital distractions, and savings schemes with penalties for early withdrawal.[65] Far from being a literary affectation, Ulysses's gesture became a central principle of behavioral design.

2. The Coherence Matrix

The Coherence Matrix is about evaluating results, but we examine it alongside Emotional Risks because it's above all an early-warning tool that detects entry into one of the five high-risk events before they cause irreversible mistakes. Spotting a fire while it's still small is a far cry from finding it after the house has burned down. Its purpose is not to maximize returns but to sustain strategies over time.

The review the Coherence Matrix calls for is by nature infrequent, typically once or twice a year, unless there are legitimate signs to pay attention to, of the kind we've already seen. Structural life changes warrant a pause, and if signs appear of a mismatch between design and psychological reality, we have to analyze what's happening before falling into impulsive sales or fits of speculation. Still, we shouldn't confuse those signs with ordinary anxiety over sharp short-term market moves, or with envy stirred by returns our acquaintances boast about. In that moment we have to repeat to ourselves that someone else's strategy may be completely inappropriate for us.

Strategies of Commitment and Other Essays (Cambridge, MA: Harvard University Press, 2006).

[65]Katherine L. Milkman et al., "Holding the Hunger Games Hostage at the Gym: An Evaluation of Temptation Bundling," Management Science 60, no. 2 (2014): 283–299; Richard H. Thaler and Cass R. Sunstein, Nudge: The Final Edition (New Haven, CT: Yale University Press, 2021); and Angela L. Duckworth et al., "Beyond Willpower: Strategies for Reducing Failures of Self-Control," Current Directions in Psychological Science 28, no. 3 (2019): 199–205.

Suppose we're in a scheduled review or we identify a reason to bring it forward. The Coherence Matrix involves three kinds of adjustment.

First, the technical rebalancing of the design's proportions. A portfolio's proportions drift on their own. For example, if we designed 60 percent in global stocks and 40 percent in bonds, after a very good year where stocks rose 25 percent and bonds 3 percent, we can end up at 70–30, which raises risk beyond what was planned. Technical rebalancing returns us to the original proportions by selling what grew too much and buying what grew less or fell. Simple in theory, but psychologically it's extremely hard: it requires selling winners at their peak to buy the laggards.

Running against intuition, forced rebalancing makes us mechanically execute the strategy of buying cheap and selling dear, which is hard to sustain by hand. Doing it periodically increases long-term returns because what strayed far from its average tends to return to it. If it rose, it grows less, and if it fell, it recovers.[66] A rebalancing alarm if some asset deviates more than a given percentage is also a reasonable option, as long as it's understood to mean marginal adjustments and not selling everything to then rebuy from scratch. If we contribute new money regularly, using it to rebalance by buying more of what's down avoids the costs of selling and all the associated discomfort.

Second, behavioral rebalancing can be even more important than technical rebalancing. Here what matters is the change in our relationship with the portfolio. For example, if we look at it more often, wake up worried thinking about swings and investments, had an episode of panic selling, or some alarmist article led us to change strategy, the design probably became too aggressive and we'd do well to think about something more conservative. It can also happen that the anxiety dilutes and the long horizon comes

---

[66]William J. Bernstein, The Intelligent Asset Allocator: How to Build Your Portfolio to Maximize Returns and Minimize Risk (New York: McGraw-Hill, 2000); and Antti Ilmanen, Investing Amid Low Expected Returns: Making the Most When Markets Offer the Least (Hoboken, NJ: Wiley, 2022).

easy, revealing a greater maturity in our signature. That means we can handle more volatility, and greater exposure to growth becomes a real option.

Third, evaluative rebalancing, which looks at the numbers, comes last and always avoids comparing ourselves to that friend who got it right or the influencer who posts spectacular gains. Evaluating gain or loss is a sensitive point, because assessing results hides a trap. The world poker champion Annie Duke named it "resulting," that is, judging by the outcome.[67] Her example is from American football, but it works for any decision. In the 2015 Super Bowl, seconds from the end and one yard from winning the championship, the Seahawks coach called a pass instead of handing the ball to his star running back. The pass was intercepted, his team lost, and the next day the press crucified him. It was called the worst decision in Super Bowl history. Yet Duke shows the decision was good. In the previous fifteen seasons, a pass in that situation was intercepted only about 2 percent of the time. The most likely outcome was to score or for the clock to stop and try again. If that same ball had been completed, the coach would have been a tactical genius who surprised the defense. The play was identical in both universes. The only thing that changed was how it ended. That means they crucified him for the outcome, not for the decision.

That's what the Coherence Matrix comes to prevent. Evaluating an investment by how it turned out rather than by how it was decided is the mistake that most blocks learning, because it rewards imprudent decisions that got lucky and punishes sound ones that didn't. In markets, where chance weighs so heavily on the short-term result, confusing "it went well for me" with "I decided well" can lead to learning the wrong lesson. For that reason evaluative rebalancing asks whether the result is reasonable for the design we chose and the context we faced. To hold that

---

67 Annie Duke, Thinking in Bets: Making Smarter Decisions When You Don't Have All the Facts (New York: Portfolio/Penguin, 2018).

question without drifting into celebration or lament, it's worth tying ourselves, like Ulysses, to the mast of three principles.

Earning little isn't failing. A modest return can be the aim of a conservative design in certain periods. If our Minimalist design rose little when there were stocks that rose a lot, that's the design protecting us against future falls. We only ask whether the result is reasonable for the design we chose in the context we faced.

Losing isn't, in itself, a sign of a problem. Every ambitious strategy has negative years by pure statistical rule. If the loss is in the acceptable range and still affects us, the problem is in the fit between our signature and the design, and it has to be corrected.

Earning a lot is, paradoxically, the most dangerous. When the strategy yields a lot, the illusion of control appears, tempting us to concentrate risks and increase exposure while dropping defensive pieces. Many well-designed portfolios break in periods of success, betrayed by euphoria. We already talked about this. If we adjust something after a good result, it should be only to consolidate gains and reduce fragility.

The three rebalancings move in a circle, feeding one another. The technical one restores the portfolio's form, the behavioral one checks whether we're still the person who designed it, and the evaluative one judges the numbers without falling into the trap of the outcome. With this spark detector, we're at the mercy of fewer devastating fires.

3. Post-Error Recovery

Most personal-finance books assume their readers will follow the advice perfectly and that if they make mistakes they can easily correct them. That fantasy makes them useless. The truth is that most people who try to sustain a long-term investment strategy will break it at some point. What do we do when, despite all of the above, we made the damn mistake? Three steps.

We start by stopping the bleeding. The instinctive reaction after a costly financial mistake is to try to recover what was lost immediately, usually by taking on more risk. This can be devastating, turning a single mistake into a spiral. The absolute post-error rule is to make no new investment decision for at least thirty days after recognizing a significant mistake. With that, the emotional activity drops and we can process what happened from a place of learning. If we sold in panic, we don't buy anything yet; if we chased a bubble and lost, we don't try to recover with new speculation. We put what's left somewhere safe and wait.

At this point we can diagnose what failed. The typical narrative points to a lack of discipline and invites us to stab ourselves with knives. Let's not do it. The character-flaw story is incomplete and counterproductive because it tait takes the eye off the system flaw: the lack of adequate protections. Calmly, let's ask the precise questions:

What emotional state were we in when we made the mistake? Panic over a market drop, euphoria over a bubble, burnout, desperation over a personal crisis, the illusion of abundance from sudden money? Identifying the specific state lets us design specific protection so it doesn't happen again.

What warning signs appeared before the mistake that we ignored? Almost never does the mistake appear suddenly with no precursors. Typically there are days or weeks of signs, like compulsive watching on the rise, internal conversations justifying intervention, maybe seeking confirmation, or anything else unusual. If we identify those signs in hindsight, they can be the basis for future alerts.

What system protection failed or didn't exist? Was there not enough friction between impulse and execution? Did we have a safety net that could stop us? Was there clear precommitment about what not to do? Did automation protect us against manual decisions? If not, we can add it.

Was the design sustainable for our real signature or merely aspirational? Sometimes the mistake reveals that the design was always too aggressive for our real tolerance and would eventually collapse under pressure. In that case. the mistake is valuable information for designing something more conservative.

Was there a gap between the needed horizon and the sustainable horizon that we didn't recognize? If the mistake was selling during a drop, even though technically we didn't need the money for ten years, that probably indicates our sustainable horizon is shorter than our needed horizon, and the design needs to adjust to that reality.

We also need to forgive ourselves without minimizing. One extreme is to flagellate ourselves, to turn the mistake into evidence that we're incompetent with money and abandon any strategy. The other extreme is to minimize by saying it wasn't so bad, which blocks learning about the magnitude of the mistake and the conditions that produced it. We need a balance between the two, recognizing that we made a costly mistake, but that mistake neither defines nor disqualifies us. The better framing: the system lacked adequate protections. We own the design and focus on what can be changed.

At this point we're ready to rebuild with improved architecture. We add structural protections suited to the type of emotional suited to the type of emotional risk involved (anti-intervention friction, precommitments), so the same mistake can't repeat.'t repeat.

Finally, the moment comes to return gradually. There's no need to do it all at once to prove we learned. The first couple of months can be devoted to the emergency cushion and ultra-conservative assets with no growth or visible volatility, if the disaster was so big that even this was affected. This lets us recalibrate our relationship with money after the trauma of the mistake without exposing ourselves to new sources of stress. Between the third and the sixth, we can add minimal exposure to growth and watch carefully how it feels. The rest of the first year we gradually increase toward a sustainable design, probably more conservative than the original design that collapsed. Better to move slowly and hold than to move fast and collapse again. After the year, we proceed with the review of the design we can sustain, keeping an eye on what worked and what still needs adjusting.

* * *

When we recognize the weight emotions carry in economic decisions, the idea of stability changes too. A system is solid when it holds up even when behavior isn't perfect and conditions turn adverse. Security, in this sense, consists of building margins that let the whole thing not collapse even if something fails or we make a mistake. No one is exempt. Before thinking about return or growth, we have to secure the basic conditions that make it possible to keep deciding without getting trapped in the pit. That's why the INVERSO Method devotes a specific step to security, understood as the foundation that keeps everything else functioning.

S

Security

When we open the phone and read the message "we detected unusual activity in your account," we feel a searing stab, and the fear of losing money mixes with the sense of being exposed. It's one of the new forms of insecurity. The way to deal with it is very different from the traditional forms, which insured certain goods, perhaps life, or simply set something aside for emergencies, trusting that work, family, or the State would arrive in time to save us if something went wrong. It was a world slower and more stable in its rhythms. Today money no longer lives only in a wallet or a bank account. It circulates through our digital identities, logins, and logins, and passwords, all exposed to decisions made in haste.de in haste. Financial security has become an ecosystem of risks where digital frauds that can happen while we sleep coexist with the old threats: unexpected medical bills, accidents, deaths, a pension system that can fall short without warning.thout warning. In this context, going on thinking of financial security as an isolated policy can leave us adrift.

Security is a framework that combines financial, psychological, technological, and pension-related dimensions, requiring systems that absorb shocks so the unexpected doesn't become a personal catastrophe. We move, then, from the internal risks of the previous chapter to the external risks, so that if something bad happens it finds us with a net.

1. Protect What We Can't Lose

Traditionally, insurance was treated as a gray piece of paperwork resolved without enthusiasm and filed without thought. Seen with a little historical distance, though, it's one of the most refined inventions of human intelligence. It may be the most successful attempt to domesticate chance without denying it exists, grounded in a subtle understanding of fragility.ty. In eighteenth-century-BC Babylon, the Code of Hammurabi already contemplated mechanisms we'd today call "insurance." For example, if a merchant lost his cargo in the river, the lender had to forgive the debt, distributing the risk. The Greeks and Phoenicians perfected the idea, and centuries later, in seventeenth-century London, merchants and sailors gathered at Lloyd's Coffee House to write down which ship they were insuring and for how much. Those improvised dealings are the origin of the modern insurance industry, which says something significant about its nature.

Strictly, at Edward Lloyd's coffee house by the Thames, sailors and merchants gathered to drink coffee and, between cups, bet on which ships would return and which wouldn't. Whoever was willing to cover the loss of a vessel wrote his name beneath the description of the risk, and from that signing "beneath" (underwriting) comes the word the industry still uses in English to underwrite a policy. Three centuries later, Lloyd's of London insures satellites, oil platforms, and singers' vocal cords with the same mechanics as the coffee house, that is, someone agrees to bear the risk in exchange for a sum we pay so as not to have to bear it alone. When the White Star Line wanted to insure the Titanic, it did so at Lloyd's, for one million pounds for the hull alone. The premium was unusually cheap, and the recorded reason is that it was an "unsinkable" ship.[68] The advertising label made the insurance cheaper. Three months later, the insurers paid the million pounds in barely thirty days. Those who had built it with their money didn't confuse brochure adjectives with a guarantee, well aware that everything that floats can sink.

The logic hasn't changed in three thousand years, but the environment obviously has. Before, the focus was on storms and accidents; today we deal with digital fraud, hacks, cloned identities, ruinously expensive illnesses, fragile pension systems, sensor-laden cars, and phones that hold more sensitive information than an entire house. In this context, insurance is less a financial product than an economic exoskeleton that holds us up when the unexpected strikes.

The insurance world has evolved too. There are personal cyber-insurance policies that cover identity theft, fraudulent purchases, or digital extortion, which in several European countries come included in home insurance. On-demand insurance appeared, activated from an app only when we need it, and usage-based insurance, where we pay according to how we drive or how much we use a service. There's even parametric insurance, which doesn't assess damages but events: if it rains past a certain threshold or a flight is delayed beyond two hours, it pays automatically,, it pays automatically, with no adjusters or drawn-out arguments. Now, sophistication doesn't guarantee quality. Useless policies abound, with more exclusions than coverage and endless fine print. It's worth remembering that if an insurance policy seems designed to confuse, it probably is on purpose. That doesn't mean we don't need them.

But which ones are necessary? Some insurance is optional; some never is. Resources are limited, and it's easy to spend on

[68]The Titanic and its sister ship were insured in January 1912 for twelve months on hull and machinery, at a value of one million pounds per ship, spread across some twelve companies and more than fifty Lloyd's syndicates. The premium was just 7,500 pounds per vessel, a remarkably low rate. The figure comes from the historical records of Lloyd's of London, which preserves and displays the original placement slip (Lloyd's, "Lloyd's and the Titanic").

unnecessary insurance while neglecting the critical kind. Among the latter is health coverage, which simultaneously protects life itself and the economic capacity to sustain it. Unlike other insurable events, serious illness doesn't ask whether we're ready or leave us time to reorganize. The form this protection takes, and whether we need to buy it privately or have it through a public system, varies radically between countries. In countries with universal public systems that work relatively well, like Italy, Spain, France, the United Kingdom, the Nordic countries, Canada, or Australia, the question is about the need for a private supplement. Most people in these countries don't have it and don't need it, because the public system covers everything necessary at no cost or with minimal copays, and no one goes bankrupt from getting sick.

Private insurance in these contexts is optional and covers things the public system doesn't prioritize, or avoids waiting lists for non-urgent procedures, gives access to a private room instead of a shared one, consultations with specific specialists without a referral, dental services, which are frequently poorly covered by the public system, or experimental treatments not financed by the State. They grant comfort, and that's why they fall into the category of personal preference.

In countries with public systems that exist but are chronically overwhelmed or deeply insufficient, as happens in much of Latin America, regions of Asia, Africa, and Eastern Europe, hospitals lack supplies, equipment is obsolete or outright broken, and waits run long even for urgent procedures, forcing people into private insurance.ny of these countries also have an intermediate layer of mandatory social-insurance systems tied to formal employment, like the union-run health plans (obras sociales) in Argentina, the social-security institutes in Mexico, or similar systems. In this fragmented system each union or labor sector runs its own health subsystem, with enormously variable quality. For formal employment they're mandatory and consume a significant percentage of the salary through automatic deduction, providing coverage that ranges from reasonably acceptable to, in very many cases, completely dysfunctional.

This model produces the perverse situation of people paying mandatorily, through salary deduction, for coverage that doesn't work,oesn't work, paying taxes that fund a public system they can't access because it doesn't work either, and then paying voluntarily for private coverage that works a little better: three systems, all at once. Of course, whoever can't afford to sustain this circus of systems is the one left trapped with the worst options. The solution, unfortunately, isn't individual. These fragmented models should be reformed toward a universal public system that works or toward regulated insurance systems where everyone has access to a minimum quality, but as long as that doesn't happen, we live with the reality of badly designed systems.

In countries with no universal public system, like the United States and significant parts of Asia and Africa, private coverage is the only option available for most. There are usually hybrid modes where some groups have public coverage, like the elderly through Medicare and the very-low-income population through Medicaid in the United States, but the majority depends on private insurance, typically provided by the employer or bought individually. Bankruptcy from medical expenses is a real risk, so not having coverage is literally betting your life and your assets against an illness. Even having coverage can prove insufficient if deductibles are high, copays significant, and coverage limits hit their ceiling during a prolonged illness.

If our situation warrants buying health insurance, the decision about which to buy goes beyond comparing monthly prices. The network of available providers determines which specialists and medical centers we can access, and its quality is worth more than a low premium with limited access to mediocre or overloaded providers. Copays, deductibles, and coverage limits can render even contracted coverage practically useless. Sometimes the requirements are impossible to meet, with premiums that come dangerously close to the value of the insured object. Policies have to be read in calm moments, not when an emergency reveals we signed whatever was put in front of us.

But what to look at? Besides the provider lists, the speed of authorizations for urgent procedures matters: it can be the difference between treatment that comes in time and treatment that comes too late. late. Coverage of preexisting conditions is also critical, because a system that allows excluding conditions we already had before signing up can leave us unprotected precisely when we most need it. Portability, that is, the ability to keep coverage if we change jobs or situations, avoids dangerous gaps. Coverage for highly complex treatments, cutting-edge medications, and and experimental procedures (which may be the only option in serious cases) determines whether the policy really protects us in the worst scenarios or only in moderate ones. We need to know all this in advance.

The temptation to take the minimum coverage is strong and can make full sense in very specific contexts of youth, health, the absence of worrying personal and family medical history, when we have no dependents, we have a solid emergency cushion, and the public system works reasonably as a backstop. But even in that case it's a risky bet, because serious illnesses don't discriminate by age and an accident can happen to anyone. The moment we discover the coverage was insufficient is the worst possible moment to change it, because now we have a preexisting condition that can be excluded or dramatically raise the cost of new coverage. We all know the maddening cases of those who discover the importance of the matter when their hands are tied. Regardless of the local health system, the functional rule is that the coverage has to be able to sustain the worst realistic medical scenario in our specific context without forcing us to liquidate investments or go into debt in a way that destroys our entire financial architecture.

Let's consider now life insurance, which exists to replace the income that disappears when we die, so that the people who depend on us economically can sustain their lives without collapse. If no one depends on our income, life insurance probably makes no sense. If someone does, it's essential. Life insurance is often sold as "investment" or "savings" through products called permanent or whole life insurance, which combine protection with a savings component that grows over time and that we can theoretically cash out. That combination is almost always worse than buying pure term life insurance and separately investing the premium difference in appropriate instruments, because permanent life policies have much higher premiums and charge significant hidden fees. Besides, the investment component typically yields less than other available alternatives. They can make sense in contexts of complex estate planning with specific tax implications, but that isn't the case for most of us.

Term life insurance, by contrast, is simple and cheap. We pay an annual premium while the insurance is in force, typically for a defined period of ten, twenty, or thirty years. If we die during that period, our beneficiaries receive the insured sum. If we don't die, the insurance ends with no cash value. We're paying for protection alone, not for a confusing mix of protection and mediocre investment.

But how much coverage do we need? It should be enough to replace our income for as long as our dependents need it. If we have small children, it can be twenty years or more. If we have a partner with no income of their own, it can be until they can generate income or access a pension. If there are large debts like mortgages, the coverage should be enough to pay them off so that the burden doesn't fall on the survivors, unless the life insurance is already built into the loan. Let's say it should be between five and ten times annual income, adjusted for the number of dependents, the expected duration of dependence, and the existence of major debts. Now, as important as buying insurance when it's needed is canceling it when it's no longer necessary. If the children have grown and are independent, if we've accumulated enough assets that our death wouldn't create an economic crisis for those left behind, or we no longer have dependents, keeping life insurance is an unnecessary expense.

Let's consider now liability insurance, which covers harm we cause to third parties, whether by accident or by failures in things under our responsibility. We're never exempt from running someone over, our dog biting a neighbor, or a fire spreading to adjoining properties. The amounts involved in damage lawsuits can be larger than the value of the goods we normally insure, and in many jurisdictions, if we're found liable and have no insurance, they can garnish wages or assets or leave us in a situation of permanent debt.

Liability insurance usually comes included in other policies, like the car one, where the third-party part is mandatory, or the home one. If the limits included in basic insurance are low, there's the option of buying additional personal liability policies that activate when the limits of the primary policies are exhausted. This is useful if we have significant accumulated assets that would be exposed to lawsuits, or if our activities increase liability risk, as in the case of having domestic employees, large pets, or properties rented to third parties.

For its part, home insurance protects the physical structure and the contents, which are calculated independently. For the structure, what's insured is the rebuilding cost, not the market value of the property, because in the event of destruction the land isn't affected, while in places where construction is expensive, the rebuilding cost can exceed the market value. What's covered is how much it would cost to have an equivalent habitable house again. As for the contents, the most common mistake is to underestimate the value of replacing it all. A useful exercise is to walk through the house estimating how much it would cost to replace what's in each space. The total sum typically surprises and is usually a multiple of what we initially estimated. Home insurance usually covers fire, theft, and weather events, but exclusions vary significantly between policies. SomSome events, such as earthquakes, floods, and acts of terrorism, require specific additional coverage.e. If these risks are present, we have to check whether additional coverage is available and whether its cost is reasonable.

If our income depends on our physical or mental capacity to work and we don't have enough accumulated assets to sustain ourselves without that income, disability insurance is as critical as life insurance. With it we cover the loss of income if we become unable to work, whether temporarily or permanently. Strictly, the probability of becoming disabled during one's working life is considerably greater than the probability of dying, but most people have life insurance and don't have disability insurance, because we think more about dramatic, unlikely events than about likely, less dramatic ones. Let's look at a curious case. In 2008, the Dutch winemaker Ilja Gort insured his sense of smell for five million euros. Gort lived from making and tasting wine at his vineyard in Bordeaux and made the decision after learning of a man who had lost his sense of smell in a car accident. The policy came with a list of clauses that forbade Gort from boxing, riding a motorcycle, or working as a knife-thrower's assistant (!).[69] Seen this way, it's the purest form of disability insurance. Which raises the question: why don't we insure our own capacity to work, which is exactly the same asset? Whatever the answer, it's worth asking.

Temporary disability covers limited periods of recovery, while permanent disability applies when working capacity is lost irreversibly. Some policies distinguish total disability from inability to perform the specific occupation, a more generous but more expensive definition. In many countries they're part of mandatory systems of coverage, whether through social security or mandatory work-related insurance. These systems typically cover a fraction of income, frequently between half and two-thirds of salary, with restrictive definitions of what counts as disability.

For formal workers with these benefits, it's worth checking what they cover exactly, what percentage of income they replace,

---

[69]The case was reported by the Associated Press on March 18, 2008, and recorded by Guinness World Records as "the most valuable insured nose."

for how long, under what definition of disability, and whether they cover only workplace accidents or also events outside work. The decision about buying additional priThe decision about buying additional private coverage, as with health insurance, depends on whether the mandatory system,re it exists, can sustain an adequate standard of living. The cost varies significantly according to our age and state of health, so we have to balance the premium we can pay against the coverage that would really protect us. If it only replaces a small fraction of our income it can be useless, and if it consumes too much current income it becomes unsustainable.

Beyond the non-negotiables, there are kinds of insurance that are critical for some people and irrelevant for others because of some particular situation. Auto insurance is mandatory as third-party liability and covers harm we cause to other vehicles, property, or people, with the option of coverage for one's own vehicle. If the car is worth little and we could replace it with the emergency cushion or by saving for a few months, insurance against own damage probably makes no sense, but it does make sense if losing it would throw us into a crisis. What's to be avoided is keeping full coverage on depreciated cars. A new car justifies full coverage, but after years it can be worth so little that the accumulated cost of premiums exceeds the replacement value. At that point, it's better to keep only liability and self-insure the rest. And deductibles? The amount we pay out of pocket before coverage kicks in is a lever for reducing premiums, but the right choice depends on our emergency cushion. If it's very tight, a low deductible can be prudent, even if it costs more.

Some jobs generate a specific risk of lawsuits over professional errors. Doctors, lawyers, accountants, architects, engineers: any profession where advice or work can cause significant economic or physical harm to third parties.c or physical harm to third parties. For these occupations, professional liability or malpractice insurance can't be missing. Lawsuit amounts can be enormous and far exceed any accumulated personal assets. Unlike other insurance where we can self-insure part of the risk, here the magnitude makes that unviable for most. If we practice a profession with this kind of risk and have no coverage, we're betting our entire net worth every time we work.

Now, as important as knowing what to insure is knowing what not to insure. There's a whole category of insurance that is statistically a near-certain loss of money. Appliance insurance or the extended warranties offered when buying electronics are a classic example. These policies are enormously profitable for those who sell them precisely because they're a terrible deal for those who buy them. The cost of the extended warranty can be a sizable fraction of the product's price, and the probability that it fails right after the manufacturer's warranty expires is low. Statistically, if we buy these policies systematically, we'll spend more on premiums than we'd save on repairs.

Likewise, microinsurance routinely pushed at checkout (card-purchase insurance, airport baggage insurance, car-rental insurance when our personal policy already covers us) is typically redundant or covers risks small enough to self-insure. The aggregate cost of all these microinsurance products can be significant without adding real protection. The functional rule is that if the good is cheap enough to replace without affecting our financial situation, we shouldn't insure it.

Alongside these two traditional categories, coverages appeared responding to new risks. Personal cyber-insurance covers identity theft, fraudulent purchases with your data, digital extortion, and the cost of restoring identity after a data breach. In several European countries this comes included in home insurance, and in others it exists as a separate product. The decision about whether it's worth it depends on how much digital exposure we have and how much sensitive information we handle online. We'll deal with that in the next section.

For their part, parametric insurance eliminates the traditional process of damage assessment and is an efficient alternative. Instead of involving adjusters to determine how much was lost, these policies pay automatically when a predefined measurable event occurs. If it rains past a threshold, a flight is delayed beyond a set number of hours, or an earthquake exceeds a certain magnitude, it pays, reducing friction and eliminating disputes over damage valuation.ation. On-demand insurance, for its part, activated only when needed, usually through an app, is useful for intermittent risks. If we use a car occasionally, we can activate coverage only on the days we drive, reducing costs compared to permanent coverage.

A bit more about the fine print. Limits and sublimits define how far the protection really goes. A policy can have an insured sum of a certain amount but then have sublimits for specific categories that completely reduce the real coverage. For example, home insurance can cover contents for a large sum but have a low sublimit for jewelry, art, or electronics, which are precisely the objects of greatest relative value. Similarly, the deadlines and procedures for reporting claims can invalidate coverage if missed. Some policies require that you report a claim within specific days or you lose the right to claim; others require that we not admit responsibility before consulting with the insurer.

We have to know those requirements and have basic action protocols ready. It's boring and it seems like we're birds of ill omen. Why aren't we out enjoying the afternoon? We can do that after fifteen minutes spent protecting what matters to us and those who matter to us. Security has bad press, but it's concentrated love. The protocols are simple: report to the insurer immediately, however small the claim seems. Document everything with photos and witnesses. Don't repair or modify anything before the insurer inspects. If the claim involves third parties, don't admit responsibility or sign anything without consulting the insurer first. Keep all communication in writing.

Finally, insurance is subject to periodic review, ideally annual, to keep the protection system aligned with our reality. At that moment we check four things. First, whether the insured sums are still appropriate and the life-insurance amount fits current family responsibilities. Second, whether there are redundancies (paying several times for the same coverage) or gaps where something seemed covered and isn't. Third, whether certain policies still make sense: a life insurance policy once the children have grown, full coverage on an aging car. Fourth, whether shopping premiums confirms the choice, since better options can save significantly without reducing protection.

Security works best when thought through with time to compare options and calibrate coverages. Insurance is one of those things bought when you don't need it and needed when you can no longer buy it. We don't want to reach the moment of asking ourselves in anguish why we didn't take care of that sooner.

2. Identity, Data, and Digital Self-Protection

Identity theft has existed ever since there were documents certifying who we are. What changed is the scale and the invisibility. Before, you had to physically forge a document; today our identity can be stolen digitally, and we may not notice for months while it's used to take out loans or commit fraud. Our financial identity is fragmented and therefore easier to copy, which is why protecting our data is nothing like tech paranoia and is part of responsible asset management. To grasp what we're up against, a single figure is enough. Cloudflare, the company that handles close to a fifth of internet traffic, blocks more than 230 billion threats a day.[70] Not a year, not a month. A day. The most curious detail is in their nature: 94 percent of all login attempts that network observes come from bots, not people. Almost all the hostile traffic on the planet is automated testing: programs running at machine speed through millions of passwords stolen in earlier leaks. Instead of a hooded hacker choosing us, there's a program testing weak passwords against ten million accounts just in case. Let's not be the unlocked door a bot opens effortlessly.

---

[70] Cloudflare / Cloudforce One, Cyber Threat Report 2026 (2026).

Modern digital fraud hacks systems but above all convinces people, taking advantage of emotional saturation or fear. OTP fraud is today the most successful financial crime in the world. OTP stands for One Time Password, that code that arrives on your phone and that in practice works as the master key to your financial life. Scammers get us to hand it over. Someone poses as the bank, an airline, or technical support and warns of a problem requiring urgent action. The legitimate system does send a code, and when we share it, access changes hands. They induced our cooperation.

Phishing has evolved to the point of being almost indistinguishable from legitimate communications. Fraudulent emails and messages copy exactly the format, logos, and tone of real institutions. The URLs are almost identical, for example, Google with a zero instead of an O, or the bank's name with an extra letter imperceptible at a glance. We should never follow links that arrive by email or message, no matter how real they seem. If it says there's a problem, we close the message, open the browser, go directly to the site we know, and verify from there. The seconds we lose in that extra step are the ones that save us.

More unsettling still is the growth of synthetic identity, reconstructed with a real document number, a plausible address, a public date of birth, and other invented data. The result is a person who operates as us and leaves traces. It's a growing form of fraud because it doesn't trip the classic alarms: there's no victim who immediately notices something is gone. Then there are audio and video deep fakes, which have moved from technical curiosity to genuine criminal tool. Back in 2019, The Wall Street Journal documented that an executive transferred hundreds of thousands of euros after a call that precisely imitated his CEO's voice.[71] Then it seemed like niche science fiction. Six years later, the technique had become far more sophisticated.

---

[71]Catherine Stupp, "Fraudsters Used AI to Mimic CEO's Voice in Unusual Cybercrime Case," The Wall Street Journal, August 30, 2019.

In 2025, a group of top-tier Italian businesspeople received calls from someone cloning the voice of the country's defense minister. The request was more than a routine corporate transfer. It asked for funds for a secret operation to rescue kidnapped journalists, which the Bank of Italy would supposedly reimburse. At least one businessman transferred close to a million euros.[72] The difference between the two cases goes beyond technology. The first exploited hierarchical obedience; the second, a sense of patriotic duty. The deep fake finds, for each victim, the exact emotional lever that disables suspicion. Detecting these manipulations requires analyzing micro-inconsistencies imperceptible to the human eye. Biometric verification companies and bodies like NIST work on systems to identify those mismatches, but the banks can afford that deployment, not us when we receive a phone call.

Another common attack is SIM swapping, an attack that breaches our security without touching us. The criminal convinces our phone carrier, through social engineering or complicit employees, to transfer our number to a SIM they control. Once they have our number, they receive all the authentication codes, OTPs, and messages, and can reset passwords and empty digital wallets. The protection is to put a PIN on the SIM and set up, with our carrier, alerts for any attempt to change the number or device. Neither is an absolute guarantee, but together they introduce friction that stops most attempts.

Social media became the highway of modern fraud, because it concentrates tired people exposed to tales of immediate success through promises of impossible returns, nonexistent advisers, fake tokens, and very strange no-requirement loans. Most investment scams begin in the feed. At the same time, social platforms are also a source of data for targeted attacks. We post where we work, what we do, who we associate with, what our first pet's name was… Data that seems harmless is often the exact answer to the security

---

[72]The case was widely reported in the international press in February 2025, among others by The Guardian and Italian news agencies, citing the Milan police, who investigated the scheme and managed to block part of the transferred funds.

questions banks use. The viral quizzes and the games of "your superhero name is your favorite color plus your first street" are frequently data mining disguised as entertainment. Don't play them.

All these variants share the pattern of allowing no time, pressing urgency and fear. If someone asks us to act NOW, we close and wait. It's always the right answer, because no real operation is ruined by a pause and almost all scams depend on our not taking one.

We can make that pause easier with a minimal risk-reduction system in three pillars. The first pillar covers six basic cybersecurity measures:

1. Use a password manager with a long master password we can recall effortlessly. Reusing passwords makes the whole system vulnerable. Passwords reveal more about human psychology than many treatises put together. For example, the most common password in the world, every year, is "123456."[73] And we're talking about today, not the nineties. It appeared more than twenty-one million times in the last year's leaks and tops the list in six of the last seven. When it isn't that one, it's "password," or "qwerty," the first keys the hand reaches for. Any program cracks them in less than a second, and yet they guard millions of accounts as we read this. Before blaming the boomers, let's clarify that Generation Z, raised with a phone in hand, chooses exactly the same passwords as their great-grandparents.

This happens because the brain detests passwords and experiences them as a tollbooth between us and what we want. Nobody likes tollbooths, and we try to get through fast by the shortest route. Who doesn't reuse passwords? It's extremely convenient until the day the data from a forum we joined once in 2015 gets leaked and that same password ends up opening our email and bank app. Reusing a password is handing out copies of

---

[73]NordPass, Top 200 Most Common Passwords, seventh annual edition (2025), produced with NordStellar from analysis of public leaks and dark-web repositories between September 2024 and September 2025, covering 44 countries.

the house key and praying nobody wants to use them. There's also the one who sticks their password on a paper on the monitor or keeps it very carefully in their notebook in the top desk drawer. For many people, a file on the computer named… "passwords" seems like a good idea. We set up military-grade encryption and write the key on a Post-it.

The real spectacle is the security rules that demand an uppercase letter, a number, and a symbol. They sound rigorous and are useless, because we all comply the same way. The uppercase at the start, the number and the symbol at the end, and the symbol is an exclamation point, because what else would it be. "Password1!" meets all the form's requirements and is among the first things anyone trying to get in will try. The best part is that the engineer who wrote those rules, one Bill Burr, came out to apologize in 2017, acknowledging that instead of making us unpredictable he had pushed us all into the same mold.[74] He himself confessed that, when the system forced him to renew the key, he just changed "password1" to "password2." When we ask the brain to be complex, it finds the laziest way to obey, which is what it does whenever it can.

2. Activate multi-factor authentication on everything we can, especially email, banks, and digital wallets. That barrier is real and most attacks fall there, because attackers move on when easier doors are available. Microsoft receives more than 300 million fraudulent access attempts a day, and the vast majority are bots testing mass-leaked passwords. Against that automated tide, the second factor is a wall, and yet only a third of users have it activated. The best cheap lock on the market is free, and two out of three people don't use it…

---

[74]Robert McMillan, "The Man Who Wrote Those Password Rules Has a New Tip: N3v$r M1^d," The Wall Street Journal, August 7, 2017. Bill Burr, author of the NIST Special Publication 800-63 Appendix A (2003) that standardized the rules of uppercase, number, symbol, and periodic change, told the WSJ: "Much of what I did I now regret." NIST completely revised those recommendations in 2017, eliminating the requirement of special characters and mandatory password change.

3. Use single sign-on with judgment. The "sign in with Google" or "with Apple" that so many sites offer is what's technically called single sign-on, or SSO, that is, a single central identity for accessing many services without creating a new password for each one. The protocol that made it possible was developed at MIT in the eighties and is called Kerberos, named after the three-headed dog that guards the gates of Hades. Today that mythological creature watches over, without our noticing, a good part of the planet's digital access.

The advantage of SSO lies in fewer passwords to create and remember and fewer zombie accounts forgotten on sites we visited once. As a bonus, we delegate the security of that identity to companies that invest far more than any of us in protecting it. Nothing is perfect, so the flip side is that it concentrates the risk. If someone gets into our Google account, they have free access to everything we connected to it. SSO is a good idea only if the central account is armored with everything else on this list, above all with a second factor. It's best to use it for low-risk services and keep separate, independent credentials for the most sensitive things, like the bank or the main email, so that a single point of failure doesn't open all the doors at once.

3. Migrate to passkeys, which eliminate the stolen-password problem at the root. They can't be copied, forwarded, or phished with a fake email, since they tie access to the device and to our biometrics. Instead of a secret we type and that can therefore be stolen, they use a pair of cryptographic keys, where one is kept by the service and the other never leaves our device and is unlocked with a fingerprint or face, so there is nothing to intercept. Apple, Google, and Microsoft launched the standard together in 2022. By 2025 Google already exceeded 800 million accounts with passkeys, and Microsoft activated them by default on new accounts. Besides being more secure, they're easier, and the success rate when logging in is around 93 percent against 63 percent for traditional methods. It's one of the few technological improvements that simplify and protect at the same time. It's worth not falling,

though, for the mirage of the perfect solution. Passkeys are much harder to steal than a password, but they don't make the account invulnerable.

The weak point is usually the account-recovery process. If recovering access just takes contacting a help desk and answering questions whose answers are on our social media, the cryptography is of little use. The same happens when we leave the old password active "just in case." Even if we no longer use it, it's still an open door.

4. Keep the operating system and applications updated. Security updates aren't optional, and the vulnerabilities they fix are public once they're patched, which means attackers know exactly what to look for in outdated systems. Any outdated device is an open door with a sign on it. The textbook case is WannaCry in 2017, the ransomware that paralyzed entire hospitals of the British health system, factories, and banks in more than 150 countries. It exploited a Windows vulnerability for which Microsoft had published the patch two months earlier.[75]

5. Beware of public WiFi. We should never do banking or access sensitive information from the WiFi of cafés, hotels, or airports. Those networks are trivially easy to intercept. There's a technique with its own name, the "evil twin," where the attacker sets up a network with a believable name, of the "Free_WiFi" type, and simply waits for people to connect on their own to intercept everything that passes through. Give a trap a trustworthy name and people walk right in. Public USB charging ports carry a different risk: juice jacking, which uses tampered chargers to copy data from the phone while it charges. We should never do banking or touch sensitive information from the WiFi of cafés, hotels, or airports; if there's no alternative, a VPN that encrypts the traffic. To charge, better our own charger in the outlet than someone else's USB port. If there's no alternative, we have to use a basic VPN that encrypts the traffic.

75"What Was the WannaCry Ransomware Attack?," Cloudflare.com.

6. Set up remote locking and wiping of devices. If we lose the phone or it's stolen, being able to lock it remotely and eventually wipe its contents can be the difference between an inconvenience and a disaster. Find My iPhone, Android's Find My Device, and their equivalents must be activated. To understand why this point matters so much, it's worth listening to a thief. The journalist Joanna Stern, of the Wall Street Journal, interviewed in a Minnesota prison a member of a phone-theft ring, who confirms that they aren't computer geniuses.[76] At first, he said, he only stole the phones, until he understood that the device was worth little compared to what was inside. He would just stand behind the victim in a bar, watch how they typed the code, and only then steal the phone. With the code in view, he unlocked it, changed the PIN and the password of the Apple or Google account, locking out the owner, with no access to remote tracking and no possibility of locking the device or wiping its contents at a distance.

The lesson is twofold. First, we have to activate the remote locking and wiping tools and understand how they're used before we need them, because after the theft it may be too late. If the thief gets there first to change the account password, those tools are out of our reach. Second, the phone code is the key to our whole financial life. How many times do we type it in public without thinking? Covering the screen when entering it, using face or fingerprint recognition instead of the numeric code whenever possible, and not leaving passwords in notes or photos of documents unprotected are minimal gestures against an everyday risk.

The second pillar refers to early alerts. Devoting a few minutes every couple of weeks to reviewing bank transactions and card charges to confirm we recognize every purchase is a very good habit, because serious frauds almost always start small and are easily resolved if we detect them soon. This is done with no

---

[76] Joanna Stern, "He Stole Hundreds of iPhones and Looted People's Life Savings. He Told Us How," The Wall Street Journal, December 20, 2023.

analysis or audit, training the eye to see only whether there's anything odd. We can add automatic tools with more layers of detection that alert us, for example, if someone opens an account in our name or alters information in our credit history. That's how identity thefts are detected long before we could discover them on our own. On HaveIBeenPwned and similar services we can check whether our data has already appeared in known breaches. Companies lose customer information with disturbing regularity, and that's why caring for passwords is a priority.

The story of HaveIBeenPwned is telling. It was created in 2013 by an Australian researcher as a personal project in the wake of the Adobe breach that exposed 153 million accounts that year. It started with five indexed leaks and today has recorded more than 845 breaches and some 14.5 billion compromised accounts.[77] The name, "pwned," is internet slang from a deformation of owned ("dominated," "finished off") born of a typo in video games, which came to mean something like "completely finished off." That a reference tool is named with a gamers' typo says a fair amount about the culture it came from. The site never receives our complete password, since it's designed with a system (called k-anonymity) in which not even its creators can see what we type.

The third pillar is reducing exposure. Criminals can't use what doesn't exist, and for that we have to make the doors disappear. We accumulate unused accounts and dormant apps when we could simply delete them and close off a potential problem. If an app asks for more permissions than we understand or need, we can look for another, and if a social network exposes data that gives us nothing real, it's worth restricting or deleting it out of pure risk economy. The so-called "Collections" compile stolen credentials circulating on the black market. A single one of them, known as Collection #1, gathered more than 1.16 billion unique combinations of email and password from more than 2,000 different databases. The greatest danger comes from the sum of

[77]IT Brew, "More Than 840 Breaches Later" (January 17, 2025).

all the sites where we once left a piece of data and that we no longer even remember. Each zombie account we close is one of those doors we no longer have to defend.

Despite all this, nothing guarantees we're completely safe, and that's why a protocol for hacks and identity theft doesn't hurt. Having the data on hand can spare us the frantic stretch of not remembering any passwords while suspecting everything is being stolen. The first hours are critical, and in the face of any unauthorized transaction or suspicion that someone has our credentials, it's worth having the following covered:

- Change the passwords of all compromised accounts and of any account that used the same password. Yes, again, a password manager saves the headache of not knowing in how many places we used the same breached password…

- Contact the bank or financial institutions involved immediately, reporting the fraudulent transactions to block cards and freeze accounts if necessary. Most banks have fraud protection, but it works only if we get there fast. The deadlines for filing claims are strict, frequently between days and a few weeks.

- Activate fraud alerts, where possible. In many countries it's possible to freeze your credit to prevent new accounts from being opened without authorization and thus stop synthetic-identity theft in progress.

- Document everything: screenshots of fraudulent transactions, suspicious emails, messages, calls, and conversations with institutions, noting what each party said. It seems overly detective-like, but that documentation can be the difference between recovering the money or not.

- File a police report, if applicable. Many banks and services require a report number to process fraud claims. Besides, if there was identity theft, it's worth leaving an official record.

- Change the answers to security questions. If the attacker has access to personal data, they can probably guess or know the answers to "your first pet's name" or "the city where you were born." Those questions must be treated as additional passwords, not as public data, and there is no good reason to hand them out freely.

Recovery takes time, usually several months of sorting out banking issues and recovering full control of accounts. With patience it's possible, if we follow the processes correctly and organize a good recovery plan that includes backups of critical financial information with an offline record of important accounts, bank contact numbers, and recovery keys for critical services, kept in a safe physical place separate from our digital devices. The recovery keys for password managers, for multi-factor authentication, and of course for crypto wallets, must be kept in a way that survives the loss of devices without being accessible to just anyone.

Most attacks look for the weakest link. It can be seen in a famous example. In July 2020, the accounts of Barack Obama, Joe Biden, Elon Musk, Bill Gates, Apple, and a dozen more figures tweeted a bitcoin scam at the same time. It looked like a movie hack and was nothing more than a group led by a 17-year-old who simply phoned Twitter employees posing as the company's internal technical support, saying there was a problem with the VPN.[78] It was believable, because with the pandemic's remote work those problems were constant. That's how they convinced some employee to hand over their credentials. The whole operation began by deceiving a tired person on the phone.

That human link is usually the weak one. So, after talking so much about risks and insecurity, let's talk about protecting another person. It can be someone close, an older adult, a not-very-digital relative, or a careless friend who'd benefit from activating multi-factor authentication or understanding what an OTP is, or, even more, recognizing a common scam. Human networks remain the most reliable security system, and helping makes us better. But even if moral arguments make us wince, we should do it anyway,

[78]New York State Department of Financial Services, "Twitter Investigation Report" (2020), https://www.dfs.ny.gov/Twitter_Report.

because looking after others also reinforces our own system. If our close circle has basic digital hygiene, the odds of an attack entering through them and eventually reaching us drop significantly.

3. Foresight and the Architecture of Autonomy

During the second half of the twentieth century, retirement ran on a simple logic in which numerous active workers financed, through mandatory contributions, the benefits of less numerous retirees with a limited life expectancy. The system was viable until the ratio between contributors and beneficiaries shifted from workable to dire through three simultaneous pressures, difficult if not impossible to reverse with any single piece of legislation.

On one side, increased longevity. In the middle of the last century, someone who reached sixty-five in a developed country could expect to live, on average, some thirteen or fourteen more years. Today that figure exceeds twenty, and for those who arrive in good health the probability of reaching ninety or more is no longer exceptional.[79] It's one of the best pieces of news in human history. We gained almost a decade of life our grandparents didn't have, something easily forgotten when we give in to alarmist critiques of modern life, especially because it reveals general improvements in living conditions globally. Yet what is good news for life is a problem for accounting, because the pay-as-you-go system was designed in an era when retirement lasted a short time.

When Bismarck established the world's first state pension system in the Germany of 1889, he set the retirement age at seventy, in a country where life expectancy hovered around forty-five. The system was brilliant in part because few lived long enough to collect it. Today the equation has flipped, and people

[79]OECD, Pensions at a Glance 2023 (Paris: OECD Publishing, 2023). The standard economic analysis of the impact of longevity on pay-as-you-go systems is Nicholas Barr and Peter Diamond, Pension Reform: A Short Guide (Oxford University Press, 2010).

draw a pension for twenty, thirty, even forty years, a stretch of life as long as an entire working career. Each generation of retirees needs financing for a longer period than the previous one. No system holds up that way.

The second phenomenon is the demographic transition toward aged structures. Fertility rates in developed economies fell steadily below the replacement level, estimated at around 2.1 children per woman, the minimum needed for one generation to replace the previous one. In the European Union, that number hit a historic low of 1.38 children per woman in 2023, and in countries like Spain or Malta it falls below 1.1.[80] If each generation is smaller than the previous one, fewer and fewer active workers must support with their contributions more and more retirees, and the ratio between contributors and beneficiaries goes haywire. In 1950 there were more than seven working-age people for each person over sixty-five in the OECD countries; by 1980 it was above five; today it's around four and is projected to fall to little more than two by mid-century.[81] One retiree to support between two active workers... The pay-as-you-go model, which works like a chain where each new cohort funds the one leaving, runs out of new links.

The third phenomenon is the fragmentation of working lives. The model of continuous employment for thirty-five or forty years at the same company or in the same sector, on which the pension systems were designed, became a rarity. Today's careers include periods of unemployment, jumps between sectors, self-employment, part-time work, odd jobs, and migrations that interrupt contributions. All of that reduces what specialists call contribution density, that is, the percentage of working life during which contributions were actually made.[82] Now, low density

[80]Eurostat, "Fertility Statistics" (February 2025).

[81]OECD, Pensions at a Glance 2023 (Paris: OECD Publishing, 2023).

[82]International Labour Organization, World Social Protection Report 2020–22 (Geneva: ILO, 2021). For the Latin American case, where informality sharpens the phenomenon, see Mariano Bosch, Ángel Melguizo, and Carmen Pagés, Mejores

produces low pensions even if the system stays formally solvent. That is, we can have worked all our lives, feel we did our part, and discover on retiring that the years of informality, the months without contributing between one job and another, the stretches of self-employment or off-the-books work left gaps that translate into a pension far smaller than expected. The system doesn't go bankrupt; it simply pays little, and the adjustment is absorbed, silently, by each retiree.

The World Economic Forum, in a 2017 report with the not-at-all reassuring title "We'll Live to 100: How Can We Afford It?," projected that the global gap between what people will have saved for retirement and what they'll really need could reach 400 trillion dollars by 2050.[83] That figure equals several times the annual GDP of the entire planet. If only it were a distant snowball, but the hole grows at a rate of some 28 billion dollars a day. The lead researcher at the WEF put it in a phrase that stuck: the underfunding of pensions is "the financial equivalent of climate change," a problem everyone sees coming, that worsens every year nothing is done, and whose cost our children and grandchildren will end up paying.[84]

Translated to a human scale, the average retiree in the large economies will face a shortfall of close to 250,000 dollars between what they'll have and what they'd need to sustain a dignified standard of living during retirement. The people who will retire in 2050 have already been born and can already be counted. We can always look the other way, but the conclusion is there looking at us. The good news is that this discontinuity condemns no one; it calls for a level of planning previous generations never needed, leaning on what's usually described as a "three-legged stool": the mandatory public system, employment-linked plans, and personal

---

pensiones, mejores trabajos (Washington, DC: Inter-American Development Bank, 2013).

83World Economic Forum, We'll Live to 100 – How Can We Afford It?, white paper, May 2017.

84The phrase is from Michael Drexler, then head of financial and infrastructure systems at the World Economic Forum, quoted in the presentation of the 2017 report.

saving.[85] The image is useful because it explains why so many people feel the floor is moving. For decades it was enough for one leg, the State, to hold almost all the weight. Today that leg has shortened, and a three-legged stool with only one firm leg isn't very stable, to put it mildly. Let's look at each one.

The first is the mandatory system run by the State or by regulated institutions. No one expects abundance, but it should guarantee a minimum floor of protection. Depending on the country, it can operate by pay-as-you-go (the active generation finances the benefits of the retired one), by individual capitalization (each worker accumulates in their own account), or by mixed systems. In most contexts, it should be between forty and sixty percent of the last salary. As we saw, the replacement rate falling steeply makes this harder and harder. Whoever depends only on it will suffer, on retiring, a noticeable drop in their standard of living. Supplementing it has become a necessity for anyone who wants to preserve some financial autonomy after they stop working.

For that we have to learn the ins and outs of our own national system, because the differences are enormous. In pay-as-you-go countries like Spain or France, the benefit depends on the years contributed and the average salary of the final years of the career. In individual-capitalization countries like Chile or Mexico, it depends on the capital accumulated in the personal account and, above all, on how that capital is converted into an income at the moment of retirement. In mixed systems like Uruguay or Sweden, a solidarity component and an individual one coexist.

Each one rests on different philosophies, which we could debate endlessly. The practical question, however, is very concrete: how much and when will ours pay exactly? Many systems today offer online simulators where you enter the projected years of contribution and the expected salary and get an estimate of the

---

85 Larry DeWitt, "Research Note #1: Origins of the Three-Legged Stool Metaphor for Social Security," Social Security Administration, May 1996, www.ssa.gov/history/stool.html.

benefit. If not, you can make a simple rough calculation starting from the "replacement rate," that is, the percentage of salary we'll collect as a pension. In most pay-as-you-go systems, that percentage today sits between forty and sixty percent of the average of the final years of contribution and has been falling because of the demographic pressures we already saw. A prudent rule, then, is to assume the pension will cover around half of what we earned while active and build the planning on that conservative assumption. If the system ends up paying more, all the better. Each country's pension agency usually allows you to check your work history with the registered contributions, and with that we can fine-tune the estimate. The more years of continuous contributions, the closer to the ceiling of that rate; the more gaps, the closer to the floor.

For that very reason, if we reach retirement age with few years of contributions or with very fragmented trajectories, we can't rely on the replacement rate over our salary, because we'll surely collect the minimum pension, a fixed floor the State guarantees that is usually well below what's needed to sustain anyone's standard of living. If the system is only going to guarantee a subsistence floor, everything above that floor depends entirely on what we've managed to save and invest outside. The sooner that reality is recognized, the more time there is to do something about it. In sum, if the replacement rate covers eighty percent of the spending we project for old age, the gap to fill with our own saving is modest and manageable. If it covers forty or less, the gap is large and demands starting early, because the only truly scarce resource for closing it is time.

The second pillar is voluntary supplementary saving, generally channeled through tax-advantaged retirement accounts or investment funds, meant to close the gap between what the mandatory system will pay and what we'll really need. Again, compound interest rewards time over amount. Small contributions sustained over decades reliably outperform large sporadic ones. For example, someone who starts at twenty-five contributing a moderate monthly sum usually reaches retirement with more capital than someone who starts at thirty-five contributing double, because those ten years of advantage multiply on their own. The scarce resource in retirement planning is time, and no amount of money buys it back.

In high-inflation or chronically unstable economies, the maxim of "saving long-term in local currency" can be outright destructive. There, private retirement planning almost necessarily runs through dollarizing or internationalizing part of the contributions and through instruments that preserve real value, because the first goal is preserving value against a currency that is disintegrating.

The instruments for this have become much more accessible and cheap, democratizing a kind of planning that used to require an expensive adviser. For long-term retirement accumulation, three types are worth a close look. Low-cost index funds and ETFs, which we already analyzed in E, are the base for their diversification and minimal fees. Target-date funds are a variant designed specifically for retirement. We choose the fund with the approximate year we plan to retire, and the fund adjusts its composition on its own over time, more aggressive at the start and more conservative as the date approaches, with nothing to touch. For their part, robo-advisors, platforms that build and manage a diversified portfolio based on the declared risk profile, horizon, and goals, are a reasonable option for someone who wants to delegate management without paying a human adviser's fees. All three make it possible to keep contributing without letting time pressure or technical ignorance become an excuse to delay.

The third pillar is sustainable supplementary income. What if we develop sources of income that don't depend on formal employment and that can continue during retirement? What comes in this way doesn't have to be drawn from the accumulated portfolio, which lengthens the life of the capital. A retirement in which income keeps being generated, however little, is more robust than one limited to consuming what was saved. Beyond the financial, a growing proportion of people over sixty-five keep some partial economic activity purely for meaning. Total inactivity creates a void of purpose that deteriorates quality of life and, according to numerous studies, health itself. As the time horizon shortens, people reorganize their priorities toward what has emotional and relational meaning, rather than toward accumulation or expansion.[86] For many, chosen low-volume, high-meaning work is a way of going on being someone who does something that matters. In these circumstances the desirable and the convenient coincide, so that the activity that sustains purpose is also the one that sustains the portfolio. Working a little in old age, when it's chosen and not suffered, protects the soul and the capital at once.

The knowledge economy makes this mode easier in a way unthinkable in the industrial economy, because it lets you monetize accumulated experience with no need for capital or heavy business structures, exploiting a very real generational asymmetry. Someone with thirty or forty years of craft in the broad sense, that of the lawyer or the doctor as much as the cabinetmaker, the ceramist, the cook, the luthier, or the gardener, possesses knowledge younger generations value and that isn't acquired in any training program, because only time gives it. That asymmetry creates opportunities for mentoring, advising, workshop teaching, restoration, select commissions, or consulting, all light on time but with medium to high perceived value, because what's paid for is the decades behind them. It doesn't happen in every field, but the universe in which it does is broad and covers all work where expertise sharpens with the years instead of wearing out, from the intellectual to the manual and the artistic. Building this option requires identifying, a decade before retirement, which of our own skills have value in reduced format and starting to build reputation in that niche through a gradual side activity.

---

[86]Laura L. Carstensen, "The Influence of a Sense of Time on Human Development," Science 312, no. 5782 (2006): 1913–1915.

It's also worth understanding that the financial trajectory advances in phases, each with its own opportunities, constraints, and behavioral pitfalls.

The twenties are the decade of time. There's plenty and it gets wasted, because at that age retirement is a remote abstraction and present bias, which overvalues immediate gratification, operates at full force. Why deal with old people's matters? And yet starting to save before thirty requires between 30 and 50 percent less monthly contribution than starting after forty to reach the same capital at sixty-five, at the same return. Sometimes ten years' difference at the start means more than double the result at the goal. The question "why think about retirement at twenty-five?" has a direct answer in money.

The thirties usually bring a jump in income along with an explosion of responsibilities. Children, a mortgage, caring for parents, more operational complexity and less room to maneuver cover everything. The horizon begins, slowly, to shorten. An investment mistake at twenty-five has forty years to dissolve; at forty it has far fewer. This is the decade of consolidating the position by cleaning up debt, calibrating risk, strengthening the emergency fund, professionalizing the insurance, and beginning to build the modest supplementary income that will pay off much later.

The forties and fifties find each person in a very different place. Some arrive with two decades of systematic saving and enjoy compound interest working in their favor; others arrive with nothing accumulated, with structural responsibilities on their shoulders and a horizon with little time left on the clock. For whoever is just starting at this point, the truth is hard but shouldn't be taken as a verdict. It will take committing a much greater saving effort to make up for lost time, on the order of 20 to 25 percent of income according to the usual calculations. If that effort turns out to be unsustainable, the answer is to adjust expectations with realism. We have to accept that retirement will be different from the one imagined and deploy creativity to build that supplementary income which, at this stage, becomes the axis of the plan. With a little optimism, it's never too late to improve the position.

When we reach the decade between fifty and sixty, formal retirement is a step away and the logic of the game changes. The strategy of heroic capital accumulation no longer makes much sense. Now we organize the available resources. In practice, it's good to reach retirement debt-free and to shift toward a more conservative portfolio, if it wasn't already, to reduce volatility. There should be more weight on fixed income and dividends, because from retirement on the net worth shifts to sustaining instead of growing. In general, as we saw, the ideal is for some kind of lifetime income to provide a relatively stable base and combine with the accumulated capital.

Before going on, let's add a warning that runs through everything else, because almost all the available theory on retirement design was born in stable economies and the world isn't uniformly so. There are two very different realities, and the tools that work in one can be useless in the other. Where everything is stable, classic planning works. You can save long-term in local currency without the value evaporating, but where inflation is high or erratic and institutions have already broken their promises in the past, you have to look for another strategy. The central defense becomes the choice of currency and jurisdiction. Internationalizing a significant part of the saving is an elementary protection. Whoever lives in one of these contexts must read everything that follows with that translation applied, because much of what's written about retirement planning assumes a world of formal employment and continuous contributions.

With that caveat made, designing retirement consists of balancing a few forces that pull in different directions, knowing that no answer is fixed. The first tension is between guaranteed income and the uncertain return of capital. The more solid the lifetime base, the more volatility we can tolerate without putting subsistence at risk, because the essential is already covered; when that base is meager or loses purchasing power, the capital is forced to cover a larger percentage of spending and the margin for error narrows. So the same portfolio can be prudent for someone with a good pension underneath and reckless for someone without.

From there follows the question of how much can be withdrawn each year. A widely cited benchmark is the "4 percent rule," which says to withdraw initially around that percentage of the capital, then adjusting it for inflation.[87] It's useful for framing the intuition, but repeating it like a mantra is a mistake, because it was born from the twentieth-century U.S. market, historically exceptional, and its validity depends on everything else. Besides, what determines whether the capital survives is the order in which the returns arrive. A sharp drop in the first years of retirement, just when withdrawals begin, does much more harm than the same drop a decade later, because you sell capital from an already-battered portfolio that doesn't recover with the rebound. A liquidity cushion avoids having to sell at the worst moment.

Added to this is the unknown of how long we'll live. Planning around average life expectancy is a trap, because half of people live longer than the average, and running out of resources at ninety because the calculations were made for eighty-two is a real risk. The classic way to limit it is to hand part of the capital to an insurer in exchange for a guaranteed lifetime income, securing the floor and leaving the ceiling free, but that tool depends, again, on the insurer and the currency. If there's a risk of bankruptcies and devaluations, an income in local currency can be a false security, and it's better to seek that lifetime floor by other means, like real assets or hard-currency instruments.

Running beneath everything else, erosion works silently, with two faces. Health expenses grow with age and spike in the final years of life, even where the public system is robust, because there are always holes paid out of pocket, like expensive medications, uncovered treatments, home adaptations, and above all long-term

[87]The "4 percent rule" comes from William P. Bengen, "Determining Withdrawal Rates Using Historical Data," Journal of Financial Planning (October 1994), corroborated by the so-called "Trinity study" (Cooley, Hubbard, and Walz, 1998).

care, which is the most underestimated expense of all old age. Inflation, for its part, as we saw in E, is a slow leak that over twenty or thirty years can halve the purchasing power of a pension that seemed sufficient the day it began. In sum, designing retirement is building something that holds up under the plausible scenarios of one's own context without demanding dramatic adjustments every time the world moves.

One hard aspect deserves a direct look. Death, among everything else it means for human beings, is also a financial event that requires planning. It seems like a topic for large estates, but even if we have only moderate resources, we can make our loved ones' lives much easier. Organizing our legacy is an act of love. Again, legal systems vary between countries, making universal protocols unworkable. In places of Anglo-Saxon tradition like the United States, the United Kingdom, Canada, or Australia, the will is the central instrument that allows distributing assets according to the deceased's wishes with considerable flexibility. In the absence of a will, the distribution follows intestate succession laws that may not match our preferences. By contrast, in countries of civil-law tradition, like most of continental Europe and Latin America, there's the concept of the "forced share" or compulsory inheritance, that is, a portion of the estate that must go obligatorily to certain heirs (typically children and spouse), limiting testamentary freedom.

This doesn't mean the will is useless in these contexts, because it serves to distribute the freely disposable portion according to specific preferences, designate guardians for minor children if both parents die, specify how specific assets should be divided within the forced share to avoid conflicts, and express wishes about assets not included in the estate. It also lets you handle situations the law doesn't address well. Such is the case of children from different relationships, unmarried partners, the wish to leave something to a charity, or beneficiaries who need special protection due to disability.

In many contexts, a basic will can be prepared with a lawyer's help at a low cost. Depending on the country, besides more formal notarial wills, holographic wills can also be used, that is, written in one's own hand, and there are differences regarding the possibility of open or sealed wills according to the level of privacy desired. In any case, at any point in life, without fixating on mortality, it's good to have that aspect of like in order, as part of the security mechanisms for our own people.

On the other hand, regardless of the succession system, some insurance lets you designate beneficiaries outside the will and the estate, without being part of the inheritance. These designations should be reviewed periodically, especially after major life events like marriage, divorce, the birth of children, or the death of a previously designated beneficiary. Outdated beneficiaries generate legal conflicts that delay distribution for years, as in the typical cases of the ex-spouse still designated after a divorce who receives a sizable life insurance payout. Reviewing designations takes fifteen minutes every year or two, while correcting mistaken beneficiary designations after death can plunge our heirs into years of litigation.

Let's also make sure the information is easy to find. Whoever is left needs to know what exists and where the bank accounts, investments, insurance, debts, critical passwords, and contacts of the financial adviser or lawyer are. Keeping an updated document with this information in a safe place known to a trusted person prevents the assets from being lost or inaccessible for months.

Finally, decisions about legacy shouldn't be a posthumous surprise. Talking with adult children, the partner, or the beneficiaries about our intentions reduces later conflicts. These situations look good in the movies, not in real families. Communicating criteria, or what's expected to be done with certain assets, makes a painful event more bearable. Even in the face of finitude, which is inevitable, we can act with composure or like ostriches hiding their heads.

* * *

Once the base is secured, the problem changes scale again. Besides protecting our net worth, we have to understand how this aspect relates to the rest of the resources that make up our life. Money is valuable, but it coexists with available time, with work, health, relationships, and the projects we consider most valuable. The INVERSO Method begins with us and has to lead back to us, so that the financial framework we built serves the different dimensions of our lives. When we think of them separately, the result is usually chronic tension, while if we consider them as parts of a single system, we can bring them into harmony. We'll devote ourselves to that task now.

O

Orchestration

At the start, in the chapter on financial identity, we looked back to ask how our relationship with money had formed and to analyze what mix of family scenes and invisible narratives had shaped our decisions. From that past, the INVERSO Method carried us to the present to understand where we are, and then to the future through goals and strategies. In the end, the present is the time we inhabit, between the flight into the past of what no longer exists and the fog of what hasn't happened yet. That present, enjoyed when we have a full life, unfolds alongside others. More than two millennia of philosophy have explored these regions, but since certain deep truths are, at the same time, fairly in plain sight, we can make use of a couple of well-known images, clear in their simplicity.

One says that adult life is made of four things: work, family, friends, and health, understood as that time we devote to ourselves for exercise or rest. We can manage two of them well, three more or less, and never all four at once. If our work is flourishing and we're present for our family, we probably see few friends and our body is fairly neglected, while if we go to the gym often and tend to our loved ones and some of our work, we surely no longer have the social life we had at twenty. The other variants are easily inferred and reflect the difficulty we all have in keeping balance. Time and energy are finite, and there's no money that buys them. The only thing we can do is think carefully about how we balance these dimensions and ease the permanent anguish of always neglecting something.

It seems like a trap meant to torment us, but here comes the second image, attributed to Brian Dyson, who was the head of Coca-Cola. Life involves juggling, this time with five balls: work, family, health, friends, and spirit, but here they are not all the same. Work is a rubber ball, and if it drops, it bounces and comes back up. The other four, by contrast, are made of glass. If one of them drops, it gets marked or shatters and never goes back to being exactly the same. Wisdom consists, then, in always keeping in mind which balls can safely bounce and which ones require our greatest care, seeking the best possible balance, that is, orchestrating.

1. Personal Orchestration

Let's begin with the title of this chapter O. The word "orchestra" is familiar to all of us. It comes from the world of music and refers to the combination of different instruments producing an effect none could achieve alone. A symphony needs a conductor to coordinate violins, cellos, brass, and percussion, marking the time and the entrance of each section without any single section stealing the spotlight. If they do it well, the result is beautiful.

The word later spread to other fields, always with the idea of a complex coordination with no rigid hierarchy, that is, one that prioritizes the whole without allowing any single part to dominate. In molecular biology, for example, people speak of "gene orchestration" in reference to the multiple genes that switch on and off in sequence during embryonic development. No individual gene "rules." On the contrary, the pattern emerges from interaction, as in an orchestra. In digital systems architecture, "service orchestration" describes multiple software components, for example, databases, APIs, and authentication services, that make an application work with no single component in control.

Let's look now at financial life, recalling the balancing of balls in which we spend our existence. Paradoxically, this book concludes by affirming that money shouldn't dominate all our decisions or subordinate the other resources. In a well-lived life, economic capital does its job by promoting the improvement of other dimensions. Orchestrating a life means adjusting those different capitals over time. Few things are as harmful as the image of a mad race after money to reach some nebulous point of wealth where we discover we're unhappy, because money was only one part.

The term "capitals" in the plural comes from intellectual traditions that pointed out that the world of what we manage isn't understood by looking only at the economy. Gary Becker, of the Chicago School and Nobel laureate in 1992, proposed the theory of human capital, in which education, skills, and experience are forms of capital in the strict sense, since they require an investment of time and money, they accumulate, depreciate when unused, and can yield concrete economic returns.[88] The understanding of economic phenomena becomes broader, since people's situations leave the binary of having money or not and reveal instead different configurations of human capital.

From another perspective, Pierre Bourdieu, the famous French sociologist, went further, arguing that reducing all capital to money is a mistake that hides the real workings of societies. Money and its variants form economic capital, but we also have cultural capital, which includes aspects like knowledge, education, familiarity with cultural and institutional codes, and credentials others recognize, and social capital, made up of the networks of relationships that can facilitate opportunities and sustain our

---

[88]Gary Becker, Human Capital: A Theoretical and Empirical Analysis, 3rd ed. (Chicago: University of Chicago Press, 1993).

reputation in the community.[89] Things get interesting when we see how these capitals convert into one another. Economic capital can buy education (cultural capital); cultural capital opens doors where social capital is built; social capital, in turn, creates opportunities that generate more economic capital. Biographies are a matter of specific configurations of different capitals and the ability to convert them strategically.

Later empirical studies confirmed that networks of trust and reciprocity have measurable economic effects. So, communities with high social capital, woven through with networks of collaboration and trust, have better economic outcomes than communities with low social capital, even if they have similar income levels.[90] Social capital is an invisible economic infrastructure that facilitates transactions and reduces costs because it multiplies opportunities.

To these three forms of capital we have to add two dimensions that contemporary life made impossible to ignore, though they aren't on the same plane as the previous ones. The first three are capitals in the full sense, in that they accumulate, are invested, convert into one another, and yield. The two that follow are of a different nature, and treating them as mere assets to optimize is one of the errors this book aims to correct.

On one side, time capital, which comprises the available hours and the cognitive energy we can devote to what, without yielding immediately, builds the future. Bourdieu included it implicitly in cultural capital, but it deserves a place of its own. Time is the beat over which all the other instruments play. Unlike money, we can't accumulate it, and every conversion among the other capitals is paid, in the end, in a currency that admits no substitute.

---

[89]Pierre Bourdieu, "The Forms of Capital," in John Richardson, ed., Handbook of Theory and Research for the Sociology of Education (New York: Greenwood Press, 1986), 241–258.

[90]James Coleman, Foundations of Social Theory (Cambridge, MA: Harvard University Press, 1990); and Robert Putnam, Bowling Alone: The Collapse and Revival of American Community (New York: Simon & Schuster, 2000).

On the other, life capital, which includes deep emotional bonds and physical, mental, and spiritual health. Here lies the true heart of everything. The real glass balls. Life capital isn't an asset invested in expectation of a return. Calculating yields in matters of love is a mistake. The moment we do, love becomes something else, poorer and sadder. It sits at the far end of the chain of conversions, the thing for which we do everything else. We can have money, knowledge, contacts, and time, but if life capital deteriorates, the rest lose their meaning.

What do we do, then, with these capitals? The answer isn't simply to accumulate them; this isn't a collection or a museum. Life is for living. Again, we have to organize them. If we go back to the orchestra metaphor, economic, cultural, and social capital are the instruments. Time determines when and how we use them. Life capital, the bonds and health, is what the music exists for and the reason it's worth playing. Orchestrating a life is putting the three convertible ones at the service of the two that don't convert. Money, knowledge, and contacts are means; well-lived time and bonds are the end. When that hierarchy inverts and the means begin to govern the ends, the frenetic race after money ends at a point where we discover too late that we dropped the balls that shatter.

Life is full of decisions that convert one kind of capital into another. Economic capital converts into human capital when we pay for a graduate degree or devote time to learning a new skill; conversely, human capital converts back into economic capital when we land a job thanks to those skills. We translate economic capital into time capital when we reduce the workday to devote time to a personal project or pay for house-cleaning services. The decision makes sense if the value of what we do with that time, in whatever capital, exceeds the cost of buying it. The reverse happens when we give time to collaborative projects or self-directed learning, converting it into knowledge or relationships that open future opportunities. Social capital becomes economic capital through connections and privileged information about opportunities and projects that depend on networks, like a job we get through a recommendation. Cultural capital can become social and economic capital by knowing the codes others recognize as valid, which give us access to networks and opportunities. The circulation happens all the time, and we can go through it like the blind or like orchestra conductors.

In this architecture, economic capital acts as coordination capital, that is, as a resource that allows reorganizing or transforming other capitals. When economic capital is extremely scarce or chronically unstable, we're forced to focus on immediate income to survive and our cognitive capacity is consumed in managing that scarcity.[91] When economic capital monopolizes decisions, we're trapped in the so-called "poverty trap," that is, in a perverse cycle where the lack of resources prevents the actions that would improve the situation. This cycle breaks only with the creation of a first margin, however small, that buys back the capacity to think beyond the day. The freed attention allows starting a conversion, for example, devoting a few hours to learning a skill or sustaining a health expense that avoids a greater harm. It also allows recovering time and presence for the bonds that urgency had cornered. Each conversion enlarges the margin, enabling more ambitious ones and opening space for what doesn't convert.

The perverse cycle, once broken, can begin to turn the other way, and that's why, since N, we've insisted on that first cushion as the lever that restores the capacity to choose. Suddenly we consider more variables and, before accepting any project, we ask whether it teaches us something or whom we're going to work with, because other dimensions began to matter besides money. We gain strategic selectivity.

While the financial strategy can stabilize and require minimal adjustments, the orchestration of capitals never stabilizes, because

---

[91]Sendhil Mullainathan and Eldar Shafir, Scarcity: Why Having Too Little Means So Much (New York: Times Books, 2013).

the non-financial capitals are in constant motion. Skills depreciate if not used, networks weaken if not cultivated, time passes with no possibility of recovery, without attention health deteriorates silently, and bonds must be cared for every day. Automating what concerns economic capital frees us to tend this complex symphony more carefully, avoiding the desynchronization that ruins the whole.

In orchestrating these capitals, each decision has its own horizon and it has to be made explicit. We can begin a course of study that takes six months and probably bears fruit in two years, which implies a medium-term conversion, or commit to a project that consumes time today with no direct return but pays off in a stronger professional network, a long-term conversion. When those horizons stay implicit, it's easy to confuse wasteful actions with strategic investment. Sometimes it's truly hard to tell the difference, but as orchestra conductors we have to be clear about it.

The multiplication of economic capital is accompanied by a periodic qualitative review of the non-monetary capitals. What did we learn this quarter that we didn't know before? What professional relationships did we build or deepen? Did we devote time to projects that matter to us or did we only work for immediate income? Did our health improve, hold steady, or deteriorate? Are we fully present for the people who matter most? These questions have no precise numerical answer, but they let us detect when some capital is silently eroding while economic capital grows.

Projection also changes meaning. In the financial strategy we projected expected returns and market scenarios. In the orchestration of capitals we project conversions and prepare them gradually instead of improvising late and under pressure. Some conversions are irreversible or very costly to reverse, like years invested in training that later isn't in demand, international moves that don't work out, or projects that consume capital without yielding anything. Conversions always carry risk, and that risk is always higher when we go in blind.

Moreover, coordinating capitals means choosing what not to do. Trade-offs are inevitable here too. Investing economic capital in one project means not investing it in another or going on vacation with the family. No configuration maximizes all capitals simultaneously, nor can it prevent conversions from operating within structures we don't control, for example, labor markets that don't value certain skills or networks that operate through exclusion. Orchestration also means calibrating those external constraints as givens we didn't create, knowing that our choices can expand the space of the possible without making it infinite. Even in the worst case, it makes it possible to detect when a capital is running out, letting us intervene before the tension becomes unsustainable.

No biography sounds alone. At a certain point, our orchestra begins to play alongside others. First comes the couple, where two systems of capitals must coordinate without canceling each other, two scores that have to become one without either losing its voice. Then, in many cases, the family, where the adults' capitals are put at the service of building the capitals of the generation that follows. Orchestration, which began as something personal, becomes an art practiced by several, and that is where money stops being a private matter and turns shared.

2. Money as a Couple

There are conversations a couple puts off for years. Money is one of them, because it touches something deep. Each person brings a financial script learned in childhood that, as we saw, is already hard to bring to the surface alone, and much more so as a pair. Worse still, couples argue more over symbols than figures. A purchase is a message about priorities and about who has a voice in decisions that matter. In truth, most conflicts in a relationship aren't resolved, they're managed.[92] The tensions emerge from structural differences between two people who see the world differently, and what sets couples who last apart from those who don't is the capacity to understand each other.

Each person arrives at life as a couple with two overlapping layers that determine how they relate to money. The first is their behavioral signature, that stable pattern of cognitive biases and emotional responses we already identified. That processing pattern stays relatively stable throughout adult life. The deeper layer, prior to the signature and less visible, is the biographical script, which consists of the learned narrative about what money means in existential terms, how a responsible person should behave, what constitutes excess or deprivation, and what role money plays in life. The script forms during childhood and adolescence through economic socialization: the silent observation of parental behavior, the explicit conversations about money at home (or their deliberate absence), and firsthand experiences of scarcity or abundance.

The difference between signature and script is subtle. Two people can share the same behavioral signature, for example, both can be Accumulators, but have radically different biographical scripts that generate incompatible emotional responses to the same situations. One may have grown up in a lower-middle-class home where scarcity was structural, while the other came from an upper-class home where the family wealth was lost abruptly through the father's bad investment, teaching that money can disappear in a day. Both accumulate defensively, both avoid risk, both prefer liquidity to return, but their emotional responses to investment proposals will surely be different. One will feel that any investment is a dangerous luxury someone in their position can't

---

[92]John Gottman, The Seven Principles for Making Marriage Work (New York: Crown, 2015); and "The Natural Principles of Love," Journal of Family Theory & Review 9, no. 1 (2017): 7–26.

afford; the other will feel it risks repeating the mistake that destroyed the family's stability.

In a couple, the behavioral signature determines which strategies are sustainable for each individual, and the biographical script indicates which specific decisions trigger intense emotional reactions not explainable by the cognitive pattern alone. When two incompatible scripts collide in the context of shared decisions, the resulting conflict is perceived as a disagreement over a single decision, when in reality it's a clash between implicit systems of meaning, so that each person defends something biographically legitimate. These patterns are worth watching in action, especially when money amplifies tensions that elsewhere stay manageable.

The couples who achieve lasting financial stability design explicit agreements that respect both logics. As in any dance, the point is to find a shared rhythm, not to move identically. Of course, there are aspects that complicate the movement. Economic power is one of them. Most couples prefer to operate under a fiction of equality. In many aspects of shared life that can be true, but when there's a significant disparity of income, the cracks appear.

Classic resource theory in family sociology holds that whoever contributes more economic resources has more bargaining power in major decisions and more capacity to impose preferences when there's disagreement, but when it's the woman who earns more, a curious asymmetry appears: women who earn significantly more than their male partners frequently don't gain more power in the relationship.[93] Instead, they compensate for their economic success in ways that preserve the threatened masculine identity of their partners, for example, with more domestic work, not less, and verbally minimize their professional achievements, in a structural response to gender pressure, even in progressive and egalitarian couples. When the association between masculinity and

---

93 Veronica Tichenor, Earning More and Getting Less: Why Successful Wives Can't Buy Equality (New Brunswick, NJ: Rutgers University Press, 2005).

material provision is threatened, men and women negotiate implicit compensations that restore the symbolic, though not the economic, balance. In intimate relationships, money carries social meanings shaped by who earned it, how, what it's used for, and the gender [94]dynamics already in place.

Economic power is also made invisible in the unpaid work that sustains shared life. If one person reduces or eliminates their outside workload to take on running the household, they generate real economic value that isn't counted in any budget. That invisibility generates real asymmetries: it erases the work of whoever sustains the infrastructure that lets the other go out and work without a second thought about domestic logistics. This asymmetry becomes toxic when it isn't explicitly recognized, though it can work well with explicit agreements. In any case, nothing is gained by pretending power doesn't exist while it operates silently.

But how to handle money between two people? Traditionally the question was posed in binary terms: everything together or separate. In practice there are multiple architectures, each with its own logic, and none is optimal for every couple or every stage of the same relationship. Let's look at the three main models.

Merged management pours all income into a common account from which all expenses come. The big decisions are made together, under a more or less explicit agreement about which expenses require consultation. It was the dominant model in single-income marriages and remains common in traditional couples or those seeking operational simplicity and a powerful signal of commitment. Indeed, couples who pool all their money tend to report more satisfaction and a lower probability of breakup, as shown, for example, by a British study that followed

---

[94]Viviana Zelizer, The Purchase of Intimacy (Princeton, NJ: Princeton University Press, 2005).

several thousand people over twelve years.[95] The impact is stronger in couples with scarce resources, where financial stress is greater and the sense of facing the problem together weighs more. Pooling money cultivates a sense of interdependence, a "we" that stays in the foreground. Couples who share finances speak of "our money"; those who separate them, of "my money" and "your money," and those pronouns, repeated thousands of times over the years, end up shaping the perception of being on the same team or not.

That said, pooling money doesn't, by itself, guarantee equality. In practice there's usually one of the two who controls the common fund, and in few cases is there equality in decisions and in each person's access to their own money without having to ask permission.[96] Sharing money tends to strengthen the relationship, provided the common fund is genuinely shared in control, not just in name. When these conditions aren't met, the model generates dissatisfaction especially in the member with lower income, who experiences the merger as disguised subordination.

Independent management is the opposite extreme. Each person keeps their income in separate accounts and shared expenses are divided according to an agreed rule, for example, half and half in absolute terms, proportional to respective incomes, or specific allocation by category where one pays rent and the other utilities and food. Personal expenses are made with one's own resources without necessary consultation or justification. This model grew considerably over recent decades, especially among dual-income couples, urban professionals, and people entering a second partnership who want to preserve the autonomy that merging finances cost them before.

---

[95]Joe J. Gladstone, Emily N. Garbinsky, and Cassie Mogilner, "Pooling Finances and Relationship Satisfaction," Journal of Personality and Social Psychology 123, no. 6 (2022): 1293–1314.

[96]Carolyn Vogler and Jan Pahl, "Money, Power and Inequality within Marriage," The Sociological Review 42, no. 2 (1994): 263–288.

It works very well for those who value autonomy as a good in itself, because each member keeps control over their resources and reduces conflict over divergent preferences, as long as the division rule is explicit and both perceive it as fair. On the other hand, it can fragment shared projects and undermine financial stability when it implies inequity, for example, if incomes are disparate and the division of shared expenses is by halves, or if it operates as a signal of distrust that implicitly prepares a future separation. This interpretation can generate emotional discomfort even if operationally the model works well.

Hybrid management combines the two previous models and fits well with the sensibility of contemporary couples. Each person keeps a personal account for individual expenses that preserves their autonomy, and they also have a common account for shared expenses and common goals, to which they contribute an agreed percentage of each income. Saving for housing or joint vacations comes from there. The rest stays in individual accounts for personal spending that requires no consultation or justification. This model has become dominant among dual-income couples in developed economies, particularly when individual autonomy and shared projects are both priorities, and its proportional contributions make it equitable even when incomes differ. The drawback is complexity: managing multiple accounts demands clarity about which expenses are shared and what percentage each person contributes. If those criteria stay fuzzy, the friction reappears in the form of daily doubt before each ambiguous expense, and the commitment is put to the test with every purchase.

Beyond the chosen model, the most common mistake is to believe this choice is made at the start of living together and stays fixed forever. We have to update the financial architecture every time one of the variables that sustain it changes. Those changes are inevitable over a relationship of decades, riddled with jumps and drops in income, career changes, inheritances, debts, children, and illnesses. Renegotiating always generates anxiety because it can feel like a betrayal of the original pact. Why change? Does it mean something is wrong? That what we chose has failed? This spiral of anxiety blocks necessary conversations and pushes couples to sustain obsolete architectures because neither wants to open a topic that sounds threatening. We have to look at the matter the other way around. Reviewing the arrangement is a sign of a living system adapting to new circumstances, not a symptom of crisis. This is especially hard in new relationships, since talking about money too soon seems mercenary or calculating, and it can be. We just have to remember that talking too late generates dependencies and expectations that are later painful to correct.

Silence has an even darker form in financial infidelity, the concealment of relevant information, which is surprisingly common.[97] The most frequent forms include hiding debts or the existence of accounts and keeping quiet about significant expenses. The greater damage comes from the breach of trust the concealment implies. Often the later revelation erodes the relationship more than the debt or the expense that was hidden. On the other hand, certain information not revealed at the start of the relationship, when there was ambiguity about what level of transparency was appropriate, becomes progressively harder to reveal as the relationship deepens. As with the review, what isn't talked about in time festers, and the longer it takes to open the topic, the harder it becomes. Financial transparency is a habit, and habits are far easier to build from the start than to establish once silence has settled in.

In sum, there's no universal protocol, but it's reasonable to have, before living together, an explicit conversation about the management model each prefers, whether significant debt exists, expectations about contributing to shared expenses, and values around autonomy versus pooling: the pillars that will shape the financial architecture once you share a home. Simply naming the

---

[97] Emily N. Garbinsky, Joe J. Gladstone, Hristina Nikolova, and Jenny G. Olson, "Love, Lies, and Money: Financial Infidelity in Romantic Relationships," Journal of Consumer Research 47, no. 1 (2020): 1–24.

topic and recognizing where preferences may legitimately differ greatly reduces the risk of feeding a snowball that eventually buries the relationship.

3. Family Organization and Children's Financial Education

Chapter I began with childhood memories. By now, the children are no longer us but our own children, and what follows is an account of how to act wisely, given that children absorb lessons about money long before we decide to teach them anything. Family financial education, therefore, begins long before the pedagogical conversations about saving or budgeting, the day a child sees their parents make economic decisions, and that's why families are the first laboratories of economic socialization.

This process, studied since the 1980s by economic sociology and developmental psychology, reveals three main mechanisms of family transmission of ideas about money.[98]

Parental modeling operates when children observe adults handling money and draw from that observation implicit conclusions about how the world works. If spending happens impulsively, children learn that money simply appears and vanishes, with no planning involved. When there's a contradiction between what adults say and what they do, the observed behavior always weighs more than the verbal instruction.[99] No amount of preaching austerity overrides the lesson of spending impulsively.

Explicit communication about money offers an interpretive framework for what children observe. When a child sees their

---

[98]C. Gudmunson and S. Danes, "Family Financial Socialization: Theory and Critical Review," Journal of Family and Economic Issues 32 (2011): 644–667.

[99]See Albert Bandura, Social Learning Theory (Englewood Cliffs, NJ: Prentice Hall, 1977); and Ashley B. LeBaron-Black et al., "Talk Is Cheap: Parent Financial Socialization and Emerging Adult Financial Well-Being," Family Relations 72, no. 3 (2023): 1201–1219.

parents postpone a purchase they asked for with no explanation, they may feel exposed to an arbitrary deprivation, but with the explanation that money is being saved for a trip or a renovation, the postponement takes on meaning and becomes an example of conscious prioritization. A word of caution. Communication can also be harmful, as when money is used as a weapon in front of the children. "Your father always spends on nonsense," "Your mother doesn't know how to enjoy" are bullets in a battle that exceeds economics, and the children shouldn't be in the middle. Equally common is the negative case, where talking about money is treated as taboo or in bad taste. A child who grows up in a house where money is never named learns that it's a murky matter, loaded with anxiety and secrecy, and drags that discomfort into their own adult life without knowing where it comes from.

Through direct experience children learn to make their own economic decisions and experience their consequences. Saving to buy something desired, spending impulsively and regretting it later, or having to choose between two incompatible options are experiences that teach more than any theoretical explanation. The impulse to protect children from disappointment is exactly what prevents them from learning to manage scarcity. The protective impulse, as understandable as it is counterproductive, leads us to spare them every disappointment. If they spent their allowance badly, we replace it; if they didn't save for what they wanted, we buy it for them anyway. Each rescue, done out of love, disables the lesson: it tells the child that consequences aren't entirely real, that there's always a net. That belief, harmless with a childhood allowance, becomes dangerous when the one holding it is an adult with a credit card and no one behind them to replace what they overspent. Letting a child make mistakes while the error still doesn't hurt is, at bottom, training them not to make the same mistake when it really does hurt.

Observation, communication, and experience together form the economic climate in which a child grows up, and we have to orchestrate that too. That means, above all, being clear about what our family transmits regarding money and its meaning. In some families anxiety predominates and causes worry and tension that lead to persistent insecurity. In others, money functions as an instrument of power, used to reward, punish, or negotiate affection. In other cases, money is seen simply as a limited resource that allows organizing projects, prioritizing goals, and building stability. In this last pattern there can be conflicts or a lack of resources, but the discussions are framed in terms of choices and priorities without trapping our children in psychological-thriller labyrinths.

The orchestration of financial education has different timings. Observation exists from the earliest stages, when the baby senses the parents' anxiety, but communication and experience come later. Consider that the understanding of exchange begins in children between ages 3 and 5, when they understand that some things are wanted more than others and you can't have everything. Between 6 and 8, broader cognitive capacities and saving skills emerge if the goal is concrete and relatively near. It's also the age where the understanding begins that family resources are limited and not mere arbitrariness. A good part of the central financial habits, including capacities as decisive as planning ahead and delaying gratification, form early in childhood, around age seven, and once settled are hard to reverse.[100] That "age seven" is not a sentence, since financial learning continues throughout life and no one is condemned by what they missed as a child, but it signals that early childhood is a fertile window we squander by treating money as a topic for adolescence.

Between 9 and 12, a more sophisticated understanding of money as a system appears, along with something new and socially charged: comparison with peers. The purchase starts to work as a visible signal of belonging, the sneaker of a certain brand or the phone of a certain model become passports to a desired group,

---

[100]David Whitebread and Sue Bingham, Habit Formation and Learning in Young Children (London: Money Advice Service, 2013).

and "everyone has it" turns out to be one of the most powerful arguments of this stage. It's the right age to build literacy about commercial persuasion, giving children the capacity to recognize that advertising and product design aren't neutral information but messages engineered to make us want and buy.

At this age a child can already understand, if shown, that ads are made by professionals who study how to generate desire, that the influencers they follow are often paid to show products, and that video games are designed to push microtransactions. It may seem as though we're breeding cynicism, but that's not what happens. Let's think of it as giving them a tool that helps them tell the difference between wanting something because they really want it and wanting it because someone invested a lot of money in making them want it. A child who learns to ask the question "do I want this or was I made to want it?" develops a consumer autonomy that will defend them, at least in part, against impulsive buying and social pressure all their life.

Between 13 and 17, the capacity for financial planning is reached, enough to think in terms of timeframes and project the consequences of using relatively complex products. That cognitive maturity arrives alongside social pressure, which at this age peaks and turns consumption into an identity battlefield, and massive exposure to get-rich-quick narratives on social media. This is the first generation that learns about money, mostly, from financial influencers, the so-called "finfluencers." Many have no training or fiduciary responsibility, no legal obligation to look after the interests of their audience, and frequently take payment to promote products without disclosing it.

At the same time, the platforms gamify financial decisions, disguising them as entertainment and pushing risky behavior through crypto, betting, or "hustle" schemes or "digital hustle" that promise passive income with no effort. The adolescent can already think in timeframes, project consequences, and understand relatively complex products. But that maturity arrives alongside two intense vulnerabilities: social pressure, which at this age peaks and turns consumption into an identity battlefield, and massive exposure to get-rich-quick narratives on social media.

This is the first generation that learns about money, mostly, from financial influencers. The so-called finfluencers became a primary source of financial "education" for adolescents and young people, and the problem runs in two directions. Many have no training or fiduciary responsibility, no legal obligation to look after their audience's interests, and frequently take payment to promote products without disclosing it. Meanwhile, the platforms gamify financial decisions, disguise them as entertainment, and push risky, impulsive behavior: crypto that promises to multiply, sports betting presented as investment, hustle schemes or "digital hustle" that promise passive income with no effort. The typical ones are dropshipping (selling products online without holding stock, which almost never works as painted), crypto trading presented as passive income, selling courses on how to sell courses, affiliate marketing, "make money while you sleep" schemes, and many other dubious promises presented as easy and almost guaranteed, when the vast majority fail or are outright traps where the only one who wins is the one selling the course that explains the scheme. The expression "predatory inclusion" has come into use to describe how these technologies expand young people's access to finance and, at the same time, expose them to scams that traditional financial education, designed for a world of stable banks and institutions, doesn't know how to address.

On the other hand, the free games that monetize through the sale of items, competitive advantages, or cosmetic elements aren't always manageable by children. Worse, loot boxes (packages containing items of random value) replicate the structure of [101]slot-machine gambling. These forms of gaming introduce minors to addictive practices without the supervision and regulation they'd have if they happened in a casino, producing micropayments that

[101]D. Zendle and P. Cairns, "Video Game Loot Boxes Are Linked to Problem Gambling: Results of a Large-Scale Survey" (2018).

can escape adult supervision. Add influencer advertising disguised as peer recommendation, and the aggressive targeting of young people for speculative digital assets, and the environment becomes genuinely hostile.

Frequent exposure to quality financial content accompanied by family participation or school education can make the difference. An adolescent who watches financial content alone is easy prey for the finfluencer who deceives them, while if they discuss it with an adult who helps them tell sensible advice from a scam, that same exposure becomes learning. That means avoiding two extremes: outright prohibition, which drives the behavior underground and leaves teenagers without guidance, and paternalism, which infantilizes them precisely when they're seeking autonomy. The middle path is accompaniment with real money that forces them to plan.

This brings us to the much-debated question of the "allowance," that is, the weekly or monthly money we give a child. Some families opt for a conditional model, where the money is given as payment for household chores done, seeking to reinforce the link between money and effort. Others prefer an unconditional allowance, as a fixed independent resource, so that chores are done as a contribution to the family without pay and the child's own money is a purely pedagogical tool. Which is better? As long as we keep the regularity, either one, as long as it also comes with conversation.[102] Parental modeling guides and deepens the experience, turning it into genuine financial literacy.

The link with household chores is less clear. Monetizing every contribution to the home can produce an overly transactional view of family life (children who refuse chores unless paid), though it works well enough in some households. In any case, some family responsibilities should remain unmonetized expectations, because children aren't employees, while the money available to them

---

[102]A. Otto, "Saving in Childhood and Adolescence" (2013); and J. Savla, Financial Literacy of Young Adults (2010).

should be predictable enough to allow planning and learning of consequences. With all that, we have to orchestrate what happens at home.

But there's also the outside. Family financial education happens in a context of inequality that children encounter in the comparison with peers who have more or less than they do. When a child asks why a friend has something we don't, the defensive answer that we don't need it fails because it usually isn't true. Let's use an answer that recognizes reality without provoking resentment, stressing that for many reasons families have different incomes and often we have enough to live well but not to buy everything we want, and we choose what's most important. It's a good opening to explore with children what they genuinely value and what they want only because someone else has it.

At the same time, there's a difference between a lack of resources and chosen austerity. A family with modest resources that explains that something isn't bought because food and utilities have to be paid teaches the reality of the budget constraint, and that's fine if it's the present situation they're going through, but sometimes a family simply chooses not to, because it values other things or is committed to a different project. Children should know this to avoid false internal narratives about the family's economic situation.

On the contrary, if we have abundant resources, challenges linked to a lack of purpose appear. Why make an effort? Financial capacities can, paradoxically, develop less if there's always someone else who solves things. Nor is the risk minor of restricting the social circle, limiting the understanding of how most of the population lives. In these cases, limiting ostentation, expecting genuine effort, postponing access to large sums, and steering children toward community contribution, paired with honest conversations about privilege, help them calibrate their actual place in society.

And what if we're in a financial crisis? In these moments, many parents don't know what to say to their children so as not to frighten them or cause them insecurity or shame. Silence, however, is the worst response. Economic stress correlates with parental depression, anxiety, and hostility, and with the deterioration of the home's emotional climate, but in cases where parents manage to maintain cohesion and clear communication, it's possible to avoid the deterioration of the children's psychological well-being and even, in the long term, it can build their resilience.[103] What must be avoided in all cases is using the children as confidants for anxieties they can't resolve. This applies especially to cases of divorce, where emotional trauma and financial complexity combine.

The destructive patterns documented in the literature and unfortunately often seen include the use of child support as a form of punishment toward one of the parents, disparaging references in front of the children about the ex-spouse's financial management, the buying of affection through expensive gifts, or sad competitions over who provides more or better. These patterns teach toxic lessons: that money is a weapon, that love is bought, that adult conflict justifies collateral harm, and that children's needs come second to revenge. None of that is responsible parenting.

One resource that recurs throughout the literature on these topics is the family financial constitution. This “internal document” can include some shared principles that guide the household's economic decisions. It should open with a statement of financial values (financial security, shared experiences, socioeconomic progress), whatever the family genuinely holds. On that basis, our constitution establishes operating rules for recurring decisions, reducing daily friction. For example, below a certain amount any adult decides without consulting, between such and such amounts discussion is required, and above a certain amount planning has to be included; we never make important financial

---

[103] A. Masarik and R. Conger, "Stress and Child Development," Current Opinion in Psychology 13 (2017): 85–90.

decisions in moments of upset, or we review the family budget at a set time and share the aspects that are relevant to the whole family.

It should also include protocols for crisis or conflict. For example, if someone loses their job, we review the budget calmly; if there are disagreements over big expenses, we order our reasons avoiding reactivity; or if expenses have to be cut, all members contribute proportionally, without any one taking on the sacrifice alone. It's the ideal place to clarify the principles of the children's financial education, avoiding the use of money as emotional reward or punishment and setting the kind of conversations we encourage at home.

It should be a living framework that's reviewed as the family evolves, to show the children that money can be managed on the basis of conscious priorities. Ultimately, this is still orchestration: the family transforming different kinds of capital into one another, and the material inheritance can be lost in a single generation, while the family's economic culture can outlast it by many.

Coda

In music, the coda is the final passage that closes a work. Rather than repeating what came before, it gathers everything up and leaves it resonating after the final note. The word comes from the Latin cauda, tail, because it's what the piece leaves behind it when it ends. A book whose last chapter was called Orchestration can't close any other way. Here, then, is the note that stays vibrating when the rest has faded.

The INVERSO Method began in identity, with a relationship to money half-known and almost always tinged with anguish, and it ends also in the identity of someone who consciously orchestrates the web of relationships and resources that make up their life. Between those two points lay a passage through quite different territory. The method's name holds its central gesture. It's INVERSO because it inverts the usual terms of financial education, setting aside the technical definitions and the rational-agent models to begin where everything truly begins, in us as concrete people who use money, with our history and fears.

Most methods promise control through technical optimization and fill us with data about the perfect portfolio and the formula that maximizes returns. It's a seductive promise that offers certainty, but it fails because it ignores the human context in which we make decisions. Others appeal to willpower and collapse at the first moment of weakness, because turning finances into a permanent test of character is exhausting and ineffective. We all fail at some point. What's the use of a method made for the infallible? Others promise abundance through a positive mindset, a particularly pernicious idea because it turns scarcity into a personal fault and confuses cause with effect, since confidence is usually the luxury of those who already have margin. The INVERSO Method departs from all three and turns them on their head, designing systems that work with our nature rather than demanding we overcome it, and rethinking along the way what we actually want in life and how to go after it, for our own good and for those around us.

Let's take one more detour around INVERSO and the turning of things on their head. According to a very old intuition, which reappears in almost all cultures, the world always comes a little upside down. The idea of mundus inversus, the inverted world, is a motif the literary and artistic tradition has repeated for centuries. It appears already in the medieval poetry of the Carmina Burana, where one poem laments that learning is in decline and the whole world is turned around, the blind lead the blind, birds fly before they have feathers, the donkey plays the lute, and the oxen dance. It reappears in the margins of Gothic manuscripts, where illuminators drew scenes to mock the order of their time: the hare hunting the hunter, the mouse chasing the cat, the peasant commanding his lord. Similar compositions burst out in the European prints of the sixteenth century, as an early form of popular social criticism born with the printing press. Around the same time it crosses the ocean and becomes folk verse and song all over Latin America, in those lyrics of the "world upside down" where everything appears overturned. Across many centuries and several continents slips the complaint of an altered order.

That persistent intuition touches something true, and faced with a world that's upside down, inverting stops being a whim and becomes a gesture of good sense that paradoxically sets things right. If the world hands us life at the margins, the means confused with the end, and anguish occupying the place of judgment, then to invert it is to return each thing to its place. The INVERSO

Method proposes, for that reason, to turn over each person's world, which always comes a little upside down.

A world upside down doesn't right itself all at once or for everyone at the same time. It goes one life at a time, one home, one honest conversation about money. Each person who does their part makes the world, in their small portion, a little more livable. But if we look up, that seemingly private matter has a dimension that overflows it. An economy is simply millions of people making decisions about their money at the same time. When those decisions are dominated by anguish and short-termism, the aggregate result is a nervous society, curiously unhappy in the midst of abundance. That's the paradox of contemporary economies, and it's stranger than it seems. By almost any long-term indicator, humanity is living the best moment of its material history.

Two centuries ago, most of the world's population lived in extreme poverty and that was believed to be an inevitable fate. Today that proportion has fallen to around one in ten people, and in just the last thirty-five years some one hundred thousand people came out of extreme poverty every day.[104] Global life expectancy went from about thirty-two years in 1900 to more than seventy today, more than double, and not only because infant mortality fell but at every age. Adult literacy is approaching ninety percent, child mortality has plummeted, and comforts that a century ago were the luxuries of a few, like electricity, drinking water, refrigeration, and instant communication, are today part of the daily life of billions.

By almost any objective measure, we're better off than ever, and yet the cries of crisis are deafening. The collective perception runs exactly counter to the data. Survey respondents in numerous

---

[104]Max Roser, Joe Hasell, Bertha Rohenkohl, and Pablo Arriagada, "Poverty," Our World in Data (University of Oxford / Global Change Data Lab), https://ourworldindata.org/poverty.

countries believe, in the majority, that world poverty is increasing, when it has been drastically reduced. We live surrounded by a sense of permanent economic catastrophe that no indicator backs up, full of a background anxiety that colors people's relationship with their money even though their material situation, measured against any point in the past, is better. That gap between reality and the story we tell reveals that contemporary financial unease cannot be explained by material circumstances alone: it is rooted in our relationship with money. At bottom, it's a problem of collective orchestration.

Without being naïve, we could say that a person who learns not to let themselves be governed by money doesn't change the system, but does change a node of the system, and a family that transmits a conscious economic culture forms those who tomorrow will decide within it. Culture, unlike wealth, spreads by contagion from parents to children and among friends who finally dare to talk about money without shame or competition. Each person who begins to orchestrate their capitals takes, on their own small scale, a little power away from the machinery of anxiety and redirects it toward what matters. The great transformations of customs rarely came from above. Almost always they were the silent sum of countless private decisions that one day reached critical mass. That's how almost all the customs we now take for granted were changed. No one legislated that we stop smoking in restaurants, or that we talk about mental health without shame: it happened because the behavior became first tolerable, then common, and finally obvious. The relationship with money can travel that same path.

Getting this far, we've already done the hardest work. What follows is a gradual and patient setting in motion, with tolerance toward ourselves, because we will fail at times, and that doesn't invalidate the method. On the contrary, it confirms it. There's no need to revolutionize everything at once or to execute the seven chapters at the same time like a master plan. Beware the grand recipes that lead to paralysis. The INVERSO Method is a way of walking, one step after another, without waiting for perfect conditions, and remembering that the difference between those who transform their world and those still trapped in the same patterns five years from now is simply the willingness to begin.

www.ingramcontent.com/pod-product-compliance
Lightning Source LLC
LaVergne TN
LVHW100310210926
848480LV00003B/1083
* 9 7 8 9 8 7 3 7 2 9 1 7 1 *